CROCHET

Home Accents in Filet Crochet™

General Information

Many of the products used in this pattern book can be purchased from local craft, fabric and variety stores or from the Annie's Attic Needlecraft Catalog *(see page 31 for catalog information)*.

Contents

PAGE 9

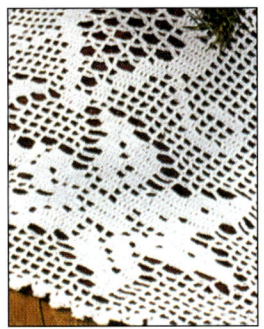
PAGE 19

PAGE 24

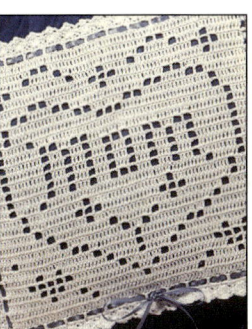
PAGE 29

Pennsylvania Dutch Set 2
Home Sweet Home 4
Primrose Scarf 5
Heart Bread Cloth 8
Heart Filet Table Runner 9
Hearts A-Flutter 11
Lovebird Chair Set 12
Floral Panel Tablecloth 14
Delicate Curtain Tiebacks 16

Grapevine Runner 16
Rose Filet Valance 18
Christmas Poinsettias Tree Skirt 19
Noel Place Mat 21
Heavenly Hearts 22
Rose Café Curtain 24
Sweet Dreams Pillow 26
Doll Collector's Table Runner 27
Mother's Day Set 29

Annie's Attic, Berne, IN 46711 • AnniesAttic.com • *Home Accents in Filet Crochet* 1

Pennsylvania Dutch Set

Design by Nancy Hearne

SKILL LEVEL
■■■□ INTERMEDIATE

FINISHED SIZES
Hand towel: 11¾ x 18 inches, excluding top shaping
Place mat: 14 x 11½ inches

MATERIALS
- DMC Cebelia size 10 crochet cotton (282 yds per ball): 5 balls #712 cream
- Size 7/1.65mm steel crochet hook or size needed to obtain gauge

GAUGE
12 sts = 1 inch; 9 rows = 2 inches

SPECIAL STITCHES
Beginning mesh (beg mesh): Ch 5 *(counts as first dc and ch-2 sp)*, sk next 2 sts, dc in next st or dc.
Mesh: Ch 2, sk next 2 sts, dc in next st; **or** ch 2, sk next ch sp, dc in next dc.
Beginning block (beg block): Ch 3 *(counts as first dc)*, dc in each of next 3 sts; **or** ch 3, 2 dc in next ch sp, dc in next st.
Block: Dc in each of next 3 sts; **or** 2 dc in next ch sp, dc in next st.

INSTRUCTIONS
HAND TOWEL
Row 1 (RS): Ch 200, dc in eighth ch from hook *(beg mesh made)*, [dc in each of next 3 chs, ch 2, sk next 2 chs, dc in next ch] across, turn.
Row 2: Beg mesh *(see Special Stitches)*, *mesh *(see Special Stitches)*, block *(see Special Stitches)*, rep from * across, turn.
Rows 3–53: Work according to chart, using Special Stitches as needed, turn. At end of last row, **do not turn or fasten off.**
Rnd 54: With RS facing, ch 1, (sl st, ch 3, 2 dc, ch 3, 3 dc) in first mesh, (3 dc, ch 3, 3 dc) in each mesh or end of mesh rows around with (3 dc, ch 3, 3 dc, ch 3, 3 dc, ch 3, 3 dc) in corner sp and (3 dc, ch 3, 3 dc) in each corner dc around ending with (3 dc, ch 3, 3 dc, ch 3) in beg mesh, join with sl st in third ch of beg ch-3. Fasten off.

SHAPING
Top
Row 1 (RS): Working in blocks of row 53, fold last rnd forward, join with sc in first dc, sc in each of next 3 sts, *sk next mesh, sc in each of next 4 dc, rep from * across, turn. *(128 sc made)*
Row 2: Ch 3, sk next st, [dc in each of next 3 sts, sk next st] across, ending with dc in each of last 2 sts, turn. *(96 dc)*
Row 3: Ch 3, dc in each of next 2 dc, [sk next dc, dc in each of next 2 dc] across, turn. *(65 dc)*
Row 4: Ch 3, dc in each dc across, turn.
Row 5: Ch 3, dc in each of next 2 dc, [sk next dc, dc in each of next 2 dc] across, ending with sk next dc, dc in last dc, turn. *(44 dc)*
Rows 6–17: Rep row 4. At the end of last row, do not fasten off.
Row 18: Ch 100, dc in fourth ch from hook and in each ch across to end, sc in third dc on row 17, sc in next dc, [(3 dc, ch 3, 3 dc) in next dc, sk next 2 dc] 12 times, sl st in next dc, ch 100, dc in fourth ch from hook and in each ch across, sl st in last st of row 17. Fasten off.

Center Edge
Join with sl st in mesh on row 43 marked with "X" on chart, ch 3, (2 dc, ch 3, 3 dc) in same sp, [(3 dc, ch 3, 3 dc) in next sp] around center design, join with sl st in third ch of beg ch-3. Fasten off.

PLACE MAT
Row 1 (RS): Ch 159, dc in eighth ch from hook *(beg mesh)*, [dc in each of next 3 chs, ch 2, sk next 2

2 Home Accents in Filet Crochet • Annie's Attic, Berne, IN 46711 • AnniesAttic.com

chs, dc in next ch] across, turn.

Row 2: Beg block *(see Special Stitches)*, [mesh, block] across, turn.

Rows 3–55: Work according to chart, using Special Stitches as needed, turn. At end of last row, **do not turn or fasten off.**

Rnd 56: Now working in rnds for **edging,** ch 3, (2 dc, ch 3, 3 dc) in corner ch sp, (3 dc, ch 3, 3 dc) in each mesh, or, in end of row around with (3 dc, ch 3, 3 dc, ch 3, 3 dc, ch 3, 3 dc) in corners, join with sl st in third ch of beg ch-3. Fasten off.

STITCH KEY
• Block/beg block
□ Mesh/beg mesh

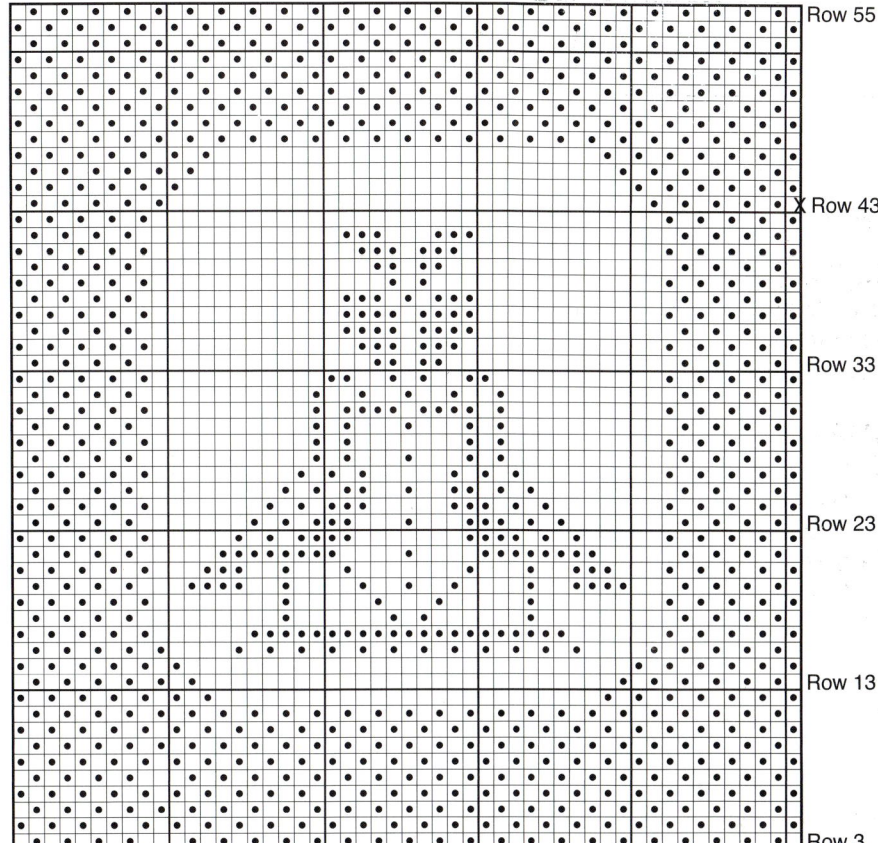

Place Mat Chart

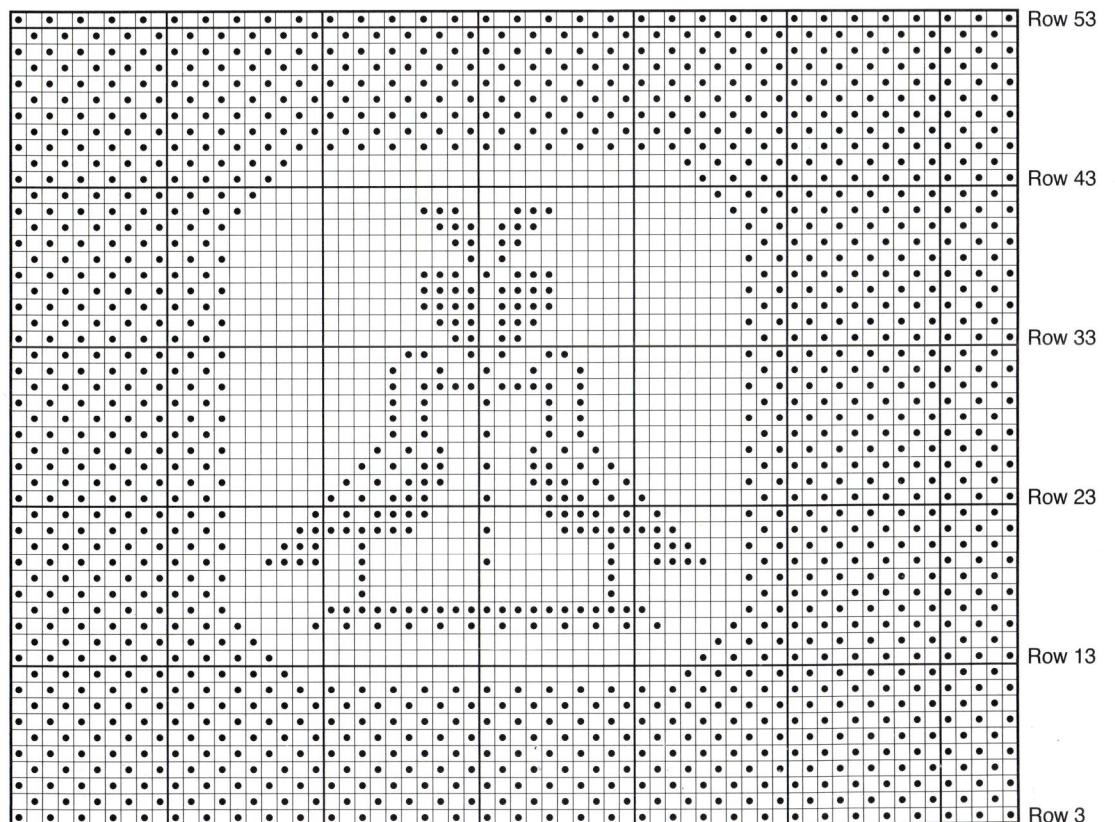

Hand Towel Chart

Home Sweet Home

Design by Carole Lindstrom

SKILL LEVEL

 EASY

FINISHED SIZE
7 x 16½ inches

MATERIALS
- Coats & Clark South Maid size 10 crochet cotton (400 yds per ball):
    1 ball #0001 white
- Size 7/1.65mm steel crochet hook or size needed to obtain gauge

GAUGE
8 sts or chs = 1 inch; 8 rows = 1 inch

PATTERN NOTE
The photographed item may contain inconsistencies in the crocheting. We have endeavored to make the instructions consistent. Please keep this in mind when comparing the chart with the photograph.

SPECIAL STITCHES
Beginning mesh (beg mesh): Ch 4 *(counts as first dc and ch 1)*, sk next st or ch, dc in next dc.
Mesh: Ch 1, sk next st or ch, dc in next dc.
Cluster block (cl block): Yo, insert hook in next st or ch sp, yo, pull through, yo, pull through 2 lps on hook, yo, insert hook in same st or ch sp, yo, pull through, yo, pull through 2 lps on hook, yo, pull through all lps on hook *(cl made)*, dc in next dc.
Shell: Working in ch sps or in sps at ends of rows, (hdc, dc, ch 1, dc, hdc) in next sp.
Corner shell: (Hdc, dc, ch 1, 2 dc, ch 1, dc, hdc) in corner sp.

INSTRUCTIONS
FILET
Row 1: Ch 58, for row 1 on chart, dc in 5th ch from hook *(mesh made)*, [ch 1, sk next ch, dc in next ch] across, turn. *(27 ch sps or 27 mesh made)*
Rows 2–70: Work according to chart using Special Stitches as needed, turn.
Rnd 71: Now working in rnds, for **border**, (ch 3 *{counts as first dc}*, dc, ch 1, dc, hdc) in first corner sp, *sk next sp, [**shell** *(see Special Stitches)* in next sp, sk next sp] across to next corner sp*, work **corner shell** *(see Special Stitches)*, rep between *, (hdc, dc) in first corner sp beside ch-3, ch 1, join with sl st in third ch of beg ch-3. Fasten off.

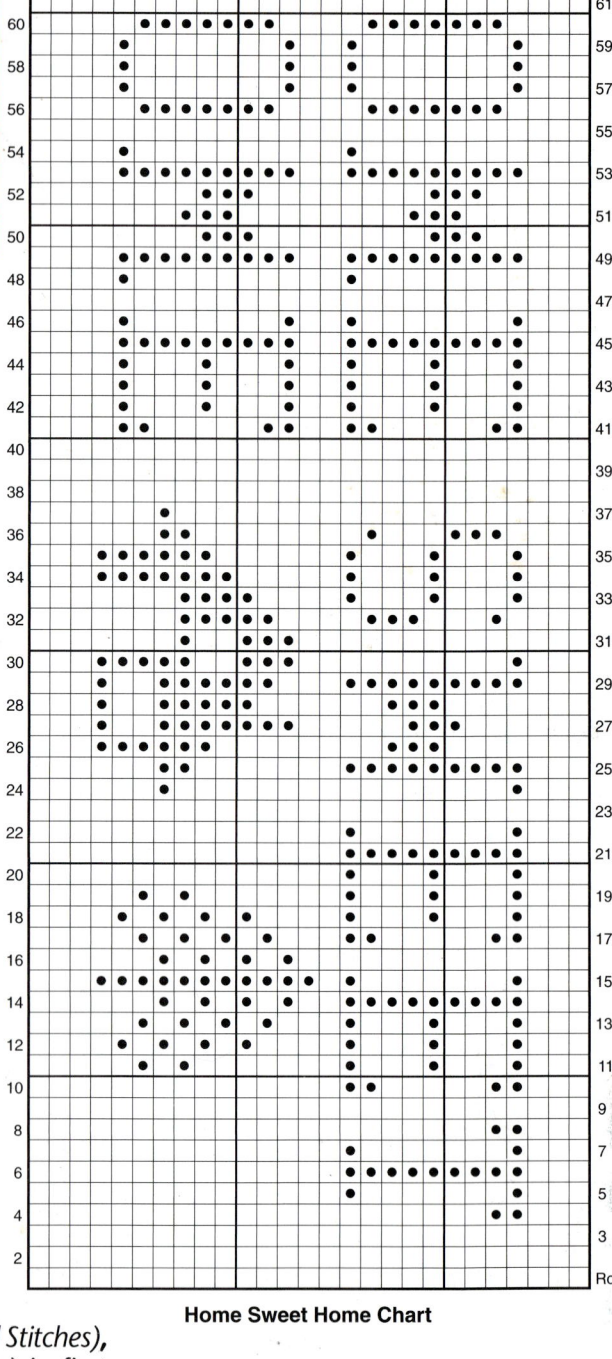

Home Sweet Home Chart

STITCH KEY
■ Cl block
☐ Mesh/beg mesh

Primrose Scarf

Reproduced from a Vintage Pattern

SKILL LEVEL
■■■■ EXPERIENCED

FINISHED SIZE
15 x 40 inches

MATERIALS
- Size 20 crochet cotton: 1,200 yds white
- Size 9/1.25mm steel crochet hook or size needed to obtain gauge

GAUGE
5 mesh or blocks = 1 inch; 6 rows = 1 inch

SPECIAL STITCHES
Beginning mesh (beg mesh): Ch 5, dc in next st.
Mesh: Ch 2, sk next ch sp or next 2 sts, dc in next st.
Beginning block (beg block): Ch 3 (counts as first dc), 2 dc in next ch sp; **or** dc in each of next 3 sts.
Block: 2 dc in next ch sp, dc in next st; **or** dc in each of next 3 sts.
End mesh: Ch 2, dc in third ch of ch-5.
Picot: Ch 3, sl st in third ch from hook.

INSTRUCTIONS
SCARF
Row 1: Ch 230, dc in eighth ch from hook *(mesh made)*, [ch 2, sk next 2 chs, dc in next ch] 74 times, turn. *(75 mesh made)*
Row 2: Beg mesh *(see Special Stitches)*, **mesh** *(see Special Stitches)* 13 times, **block** *(see Special Stitches)* 4 times, mesh 14 times, block 10 times, mesh 3 times, block twice, mesh 10 times, block 4 times, mesh 13 times, **end mesh** *(see Special Stitches)*, turn.
Row 3: Beg mesh, mesh 12 times, block, mesh 4 times, block, mesh 11 times, block, mesh 2 times, block 4 times, mesh, block 6 times, mesh 12 times, block, mesh 4 times, block, mesh 12 times, end mesh, turn.
Rows 4–241: Work according to chart, using Special Stitches as needed. At end of last row, **do not fasten off.**

EDGING
Ch 3, 2 dc in corner mesh, *ch 4, sk next mesh, sc in next mesh, ch 4, sk next mesh, 3 dc in next mesh, **picot** *(see Special Stitches)*, 3 dc in next mesh, ch 4, sk next mesh, sc in next mesh across to corner**, ch 4, (3 dc, picot, 3 dc) in corner sp, working in ends of rows, starting ch on opposite side of row 1, rep from * around, ending last rep at **, ch 4, 3 dc in same mesh as first dc, picot, join with sl st in third ch of beg ch-3. Fasten off.❑❑

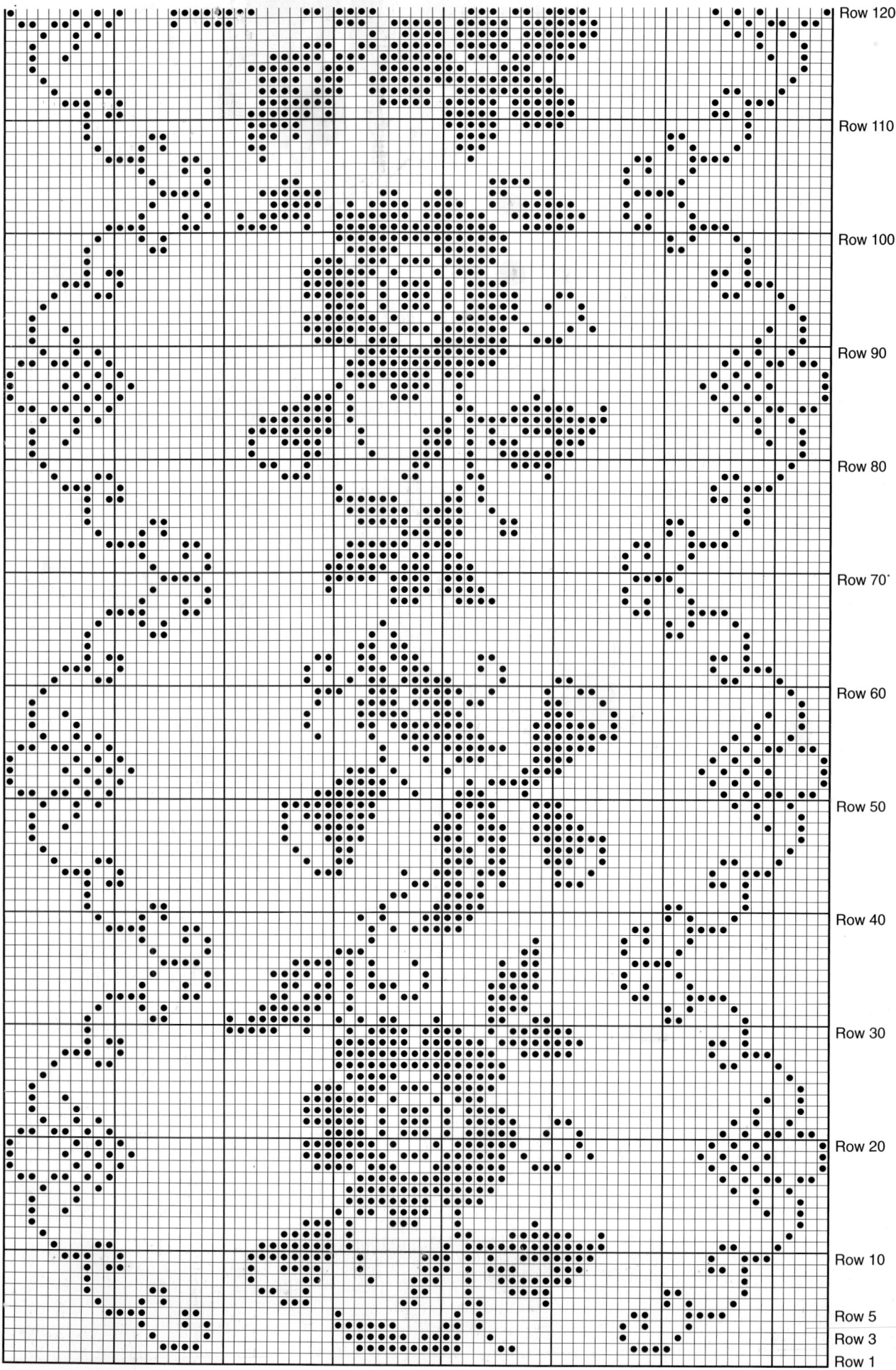

Primrose Scarf Chart
Left Side

STITCH KEY
- ☐ Beg mesh/mesh/end mesh
- ● Beg block/block

Row 240
Row 230
Row 220
Row 210
Row 200
Row 190
Row 180
Row 170
Row 160
Row 150
Row 140
Row 130
Row 121

Primrose Scarf Chart
Right Side

Heart Bread Cloth

Design by Dot Drake

SKILL LEVEL
■■■□ INTERMEDIATE

FINISHED SIZE
13 inches square

MATERIALS
- J.&P. Coats Big Ball size 20 crochet cotton (400 yds per ball)
  1 ball #0001 white
- Size 9/1.25mm steel crochet hook or size needed to obtain gauge

GAUGE
13 sts or chs = 1 inch; 9 rows = 2 inches

SPECIAL STITCHES
Beginning mesh (beg mesh): Ch 5 *(counts as first dc and ch 2)*, sk next 2 sts; **or** chs, dc in next st.

Mesh: Ch 2, sk next 2 sts or chs, dc in next st.

Beginning block (beg block): Ch 3 *(counts as first dc)*, dc in each of next 3 sts; **or**, ch 3, 2 dc in next ch sp, dc in next dc.

Block: Dc in each of next 3 sts; **or**, 2 dc in next ch sp, dc in next st.

Corner block: Ch 3, 2 dc around side of last dc made, dc again in last worked st on last rnd.

Corner mesh: Ch 2, dc in top of ch-3 of corner block.

INSTRUCTIONS
BREAD CLOTH
Row 1: Ch 110, for row 1 of graph, dc in eighth ch from hook *(first beg mesh made)*, **block** *(see Special Stitches)* twice, **mesh** *(see Special Stitches)* across to last 9 chs, block twice, mesh, turn. *(35 blocks and mesh made)*

Rows 2–35: Work according to chart, using Special Stitches as needed, turn. At end of last row, **do not turn**.

Row 36: For **border**, (ch 6—*counts as first dc and ch-3*, dc) in last dc on row 35, working in tops of sts at end of rows, [ch 2, dc in next row] across to corner, (ch 2, dc, ch 3, dc) in corner, working in starting ch on opposite side of row 1, [ch 2, sk next 2 chs, dc in next ch] across to corner, (ch 2, dc, ch 3, dc) in corner, working tops of sts at ends of rows, ch 2, dc in row 1, [ch 2, dc in next row] across to corner, (ch 2, dc, ch 3, dc) in corner, working across row 35, [ch 2, sk next 2 sts or chs, dc in next st] across, sk last 2 sts or ch, ch 2, join with sl st in third ch of beg ch-6.

Rnd 37: Now working in rnds, ch 3, 5 dc in each corner sp with 2 dc in each ch-2 sp and dc in each dc around, join with sl st in third ch of beg ch-3.

Rnd 38: Sl st in each of next 2 dc, (ch 5, dc) in next dc, *ch 2, sk next 2 dc, [dc in next dc, ch 2, sk next 2 dc] across** to center dc of 5-dc group at next corner, (dc, ch 3, dc) in center dc, rep from * around, ending last rep at **, join with sl st in third ch of beg ch-5.

Rnd 39: Sl st in next ch, (sl st, ch 5, dc) in next ch, mesh around with (ch 2, dc, ch 3, dc) in second ch of each corner ch-3 sp, ending with ch 2, join.

Rnd 40: Rep rnd 37.

Rnd 41: Sl st in each of next 3 chs, **beg mesh** *(see Special Stitches)*, [block, mesh] 20 times, **corner**

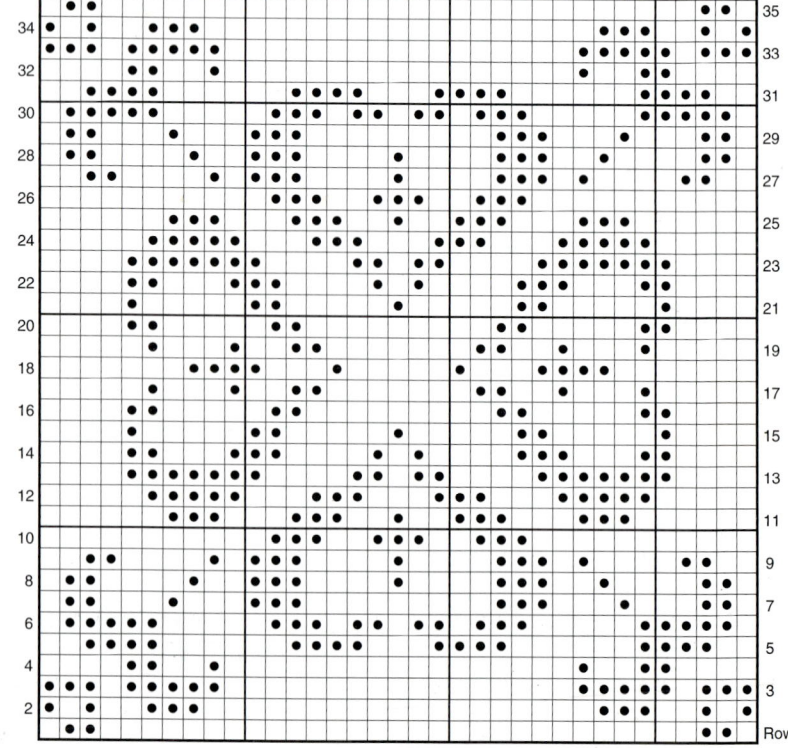

STITCH KEY
- ■ Block/beg block
- □ Mesh/beg mesh

Bread Cloth Chart

8 • *Home Accents in Filet Crochet* • Annie's Attic, Berne, IN 46711 • AnniesAttic.com

block *(see Special Stitches)*, *mesh, [block, mesh] 20 times**, corner block, rep from * around, ending last rep at **, ch 3, 2 dc around side of last dc made, join.

Rnd 42: **Beg block** *(see Special Stitches)*, [mesh, block] across to next corner block, **corner mesh** *(see Special Stitches)*, work corner block, [mesh, block] across to next corner block, work corner mesh, rep from * 3 times, ch 3, 2 dc around side of last dc made, join.

Rnd 43: Beg mesh, block, *[mesh, block] across to next corner block, work corner mesh, corner block, rep from * 3 times, mesh, 2 dc in last ch sp, join.

Rnd 44: Beg block, *[mesh, block] across to next corner block, work corner mesh, corner block, rep from * 3 times, mesh, block, ch 2, join.

Rnd 45: Ch 3, *dc in each st and 2 dc in each ch sp across to next corner block, dc in each ch of ch-3 at beg of corner block, ch 3, 2 dc around side of last dc made, rep from * 3 times, dc in each st and 2 dc in each ch sp across, join.

Rnd 46: Working in sts and in chs at beg of corner blocks, *ch 2, sk next 2 sts or chs, (2 dc, ch 3, sc in third ch from hook, 2 dc) in next st or ch, ch 2, sk next 2 sts or chs, sc in next st or ch, rep from * around *(sk only one st or ch at corners if needed for edge to lie flat or if needed for last rep to end evenly)*, join with sl st in first ch of beg ch-2. Fasten off.❑❑

Heart Filet Table Runner

Design by Dot Drake

SKILL LEVEL
■■□□ EASY

FINISHED SIZE
13 x 39 inches

MATERIALS
❑ Aunt Lydia's Special Value size 10 crochet cotton (1000 yds per ball):
   1 ball #0201 white
❑ Size 8/1.50mm steel crochet hook or size needed to obtain gauge

GAUGE
12 sts or chs = 1 inch; 9 rows = 2 inches

SPECIAL STITCHES
Beginning block (beg block): Ch 3 *(counts as first dc)*, dc in next 3 sts; **or,** ch 3, 2 dc in next ch sp, dc in next dc.
Block: Dc in next 3 sts; **or,** 2 dc in next ch sp, dc in next dc.
Mesh: Ch 2, sk next 2 sts or chs, dc in next st.
Double mesh: Ch 5, sk next 5 sts or chs, dc in next dc **or** in center ch of ch sp.
Shell: (3 dc, ch 5, 3 dc) in next st or ch.
Picot: Ch 4, sl st in third ch from hook, ch 1.
Triple crochet decrease (tr dec): *Yo twice, insert as specified, yo, pull lp through, [yo, pull through 2 lps on hook] twice, rep from *, yo, pull through all lps on hook.

INSTRUCTIONS
TABLE RUNNER
Row 1: Ch 126, for row 1 of graph, dc in fourth ch from hook *(first 3 chs count as first dc)* and in each ch across, turn. *(124 dc made)*
Rows 2–81: Work according to chart, using Special Stitches as needed, turn.
Rows 82–161: Turn chart around and work row 80 to row 1 in reverse order. At end of last row, **do not turn.**

BORDER

Rnd 1: Now working in rnds, (ch 3, 2 dc, ch 5, 3 dc) in last dc on row 161; work the following steps to complete rnd;

A: Working in tops of sts at end of rows, sk row 160, **shell** *(see Special Stitches)* in next row, [sk same row and next 2 rows, shell in next row] across with last shell in top of row 3;

B: Working in starting ch on opposite side of row 1, shell in first ch, [sk next 5 chs, shell in next ch] twice, [sk next 6 chs, shell in next ch] across to last 12 chs before next corner, [sk next 5 chs, shell in next ch] twice with last shell in corner ch;

C: Working in tops of sts at ends of rows, shell in row 2, [sk next 2 rows, shell in next row] across with last shell in top of corner st on row 161;

D: [Sk next 5 sts, shell in next st] twice, [sk next 6 sts, shell in next st] 14 times, sk next 5 sts, shell in next st, sk next 5 sts, join with sl st in third ch of beg ch-3.

Rnd 2: Sl st across to next ch-5 sp, (sl st, ch 5—*counts as first tr and ch-1*, tr) in ch sp, (ch 1, tr) 7 times in same ch sp *(first scallop made)*, ch 2, (sc, ch 3, sc) in next ch sp, ch 2, *[tr in next ch sp, (ch 1, tr) 6 times in same ch sp as last tr made *(next scallop made)*, ch 2, (sc, ch 3, sc) in next ch sp, ch 2]** across to next corner, tr in corner ch sp, (ch 1, tr) 8 times in same corner ch sp *(next scallop made)*, ch 2, (sc, ch 3, sc) in next ch sp, ch 2, rep from * around, ending last rep at **, join with sl st in fourth ch of beg ch-5.

Rnd 3: Ch 4 *(counts as first tr)*, sk each ch sp, tr in next tr, [**picot** *(see Special Stitches)*, **tr dec** *(see Special Stitches)* in last worked tr and next tr] 7 times across first scallop, ch 4, picot, *working across next scallop, tr dec in next 2 tr, [picot, tr dec in last tr worked in and next tr] across scallop, ch 4, picot, rep from * around, join in fourth ch of beg ch-4. Fasten off.

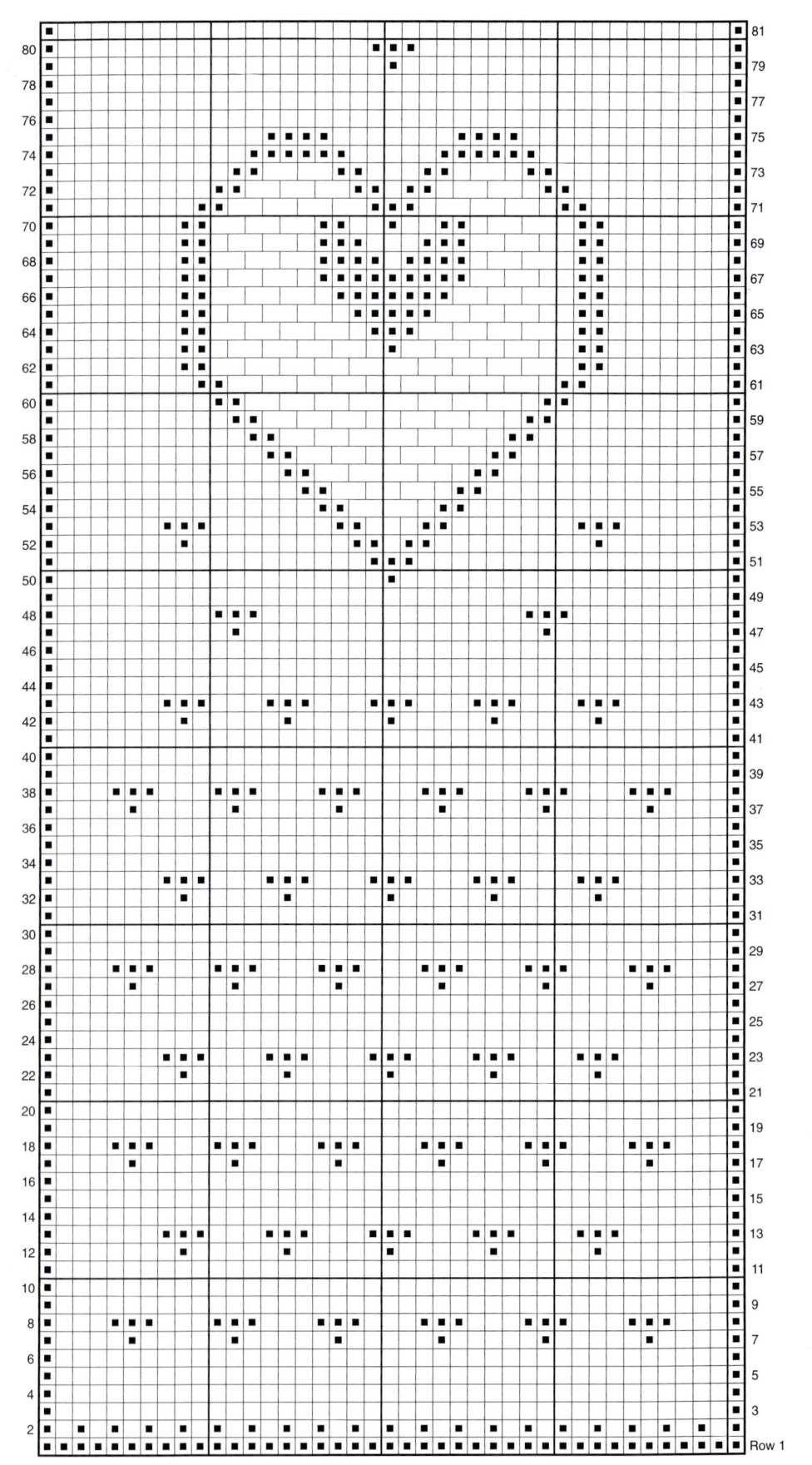

Heart Filet Chart

STITCH KEY
■ Beg block/block
☐ Mesh
☐ Double mesh

Hearts A-Flutter

Design by Vicki Blizzard

SKILL LEVEL
 EASY

FINISHED SIZE
50 x 16½ inches

MATERIALS
- DMC Cebelia size 10 crochet cotton (285 yds per ball): 4 balls #224 very light shell pink
- Size 7/1.65mm steel crochet hook or size needed to obtain gauge

GAUGE
10 dc = 1 inch; 8 rows = 2 inches

SPECIAL STITCHES
Mesh: Ch 2, sk next 2 sts or chs, dc in next st.
Block: Dc in each of next 3 sts; **or** 2 dc in next ch-2 sp, dc in next st.
Beginning block (beg block): Ch 3 *(counts as first dc)*, dc in each of next 3 dc.
Extended treble crochet (xtr): Yo 6 times, pull up lp in indicated st, [yo, pull through 2 lps on hook] 7 times.

INSTRUCTIONS
VALANCE
Row 1 (RS): Beg at top, ch 411, dc in fourth ch *(first 3 chs count as first dc)* from hook and in each ch across, turn. (409 dc made)
Rows 2–42: Beg block *(see Special Stitches)*, mesh *(see Special Stitches)* across to last 3 sts, block *(see Special Stitches)*, turn. (134 ch-2 sps)
Rows 43–62: Work according to chart across, using Special Stitches as needed, turn. At end of last row, fasten off.

ROD POCKET
Row 1: With WS facing, working starting ch on opposite side of row 1, join with sl st in first ch, ch 12 *(counts as first xtr, ch 2)*, sk next 2 chs, **xtr** *(see Special Stitches)* in next ch, [ch 2, sk next 2 chs, xtr in next ch] across, turn.
Row 2: Ch 3, 2 dc in first ch-2 sp, [dc in next dc, 2 dc in next ch-2 sp] across, ending with dc in last st. Fasten off.

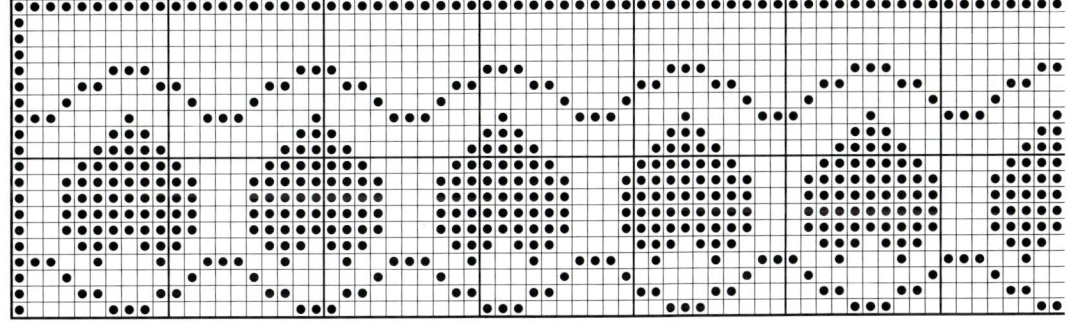

Hearts A-Flutter Chart
Left Side

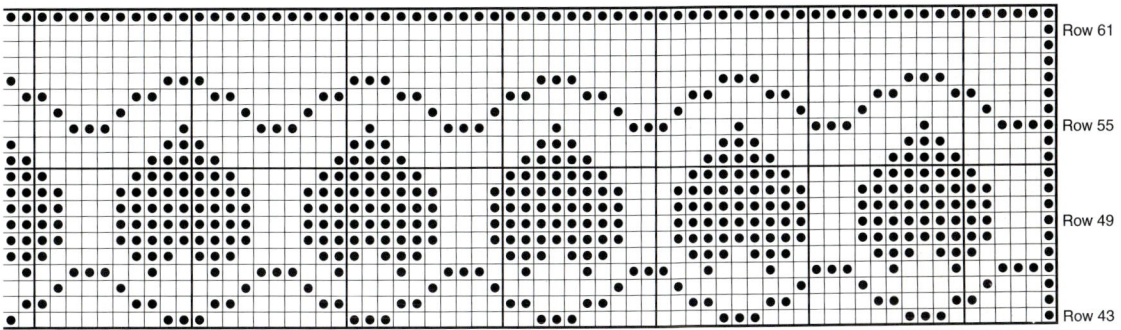

Hearts A-Flutter Chart
Right Side

STITCH KEY
☐ Mesh
● Block/beg block

Lovebird Chair Set

Design by Alice Gundel

SKILL LEVEL
■■■□ INTERMEDIATE

FINISHED SIZES
Arm piece: 11 x 16 inches
Chair back: 16½ x 26 inches

MATERIALS
- J.&P. Coats Knit-Cro-Sheen size 10 crochet cotton (225 yds per ball):
    3 balls #61 ecru (arm piece)
    4 balls #61 ecru (chair back)
- Size 6/1.80mm steel crochet hook or size needed to obtain gauge

STITCH KEY
- ▪ Block
- ☐ Mesh/beg mesh
- ⊟ Double mesh
- ⌵ Lacet

GAUGE
5 dc = ½ inch; 2 dc rows = ½ inch

SPECIAL STITCHES
Beginning mesh (beg mesh): Ch 5 (counts as first dc and ch 2), dc in next dc.
Mesh: Ch 2, sk next 2 sts or chs, dc in next st or ch.
Block: 2 dc in next ch sp, dc in next st; **or,** dc in each of next 3 sts.
Lacet: Ch 3, sk next 2 sts or ch sp, sc in next st, ch 3, sk next 2 sts or ch sp, dc in next dc.
Double mesh: Ch 5, sk next sc, dc in next dc.

INSTRUCTIONS
CHAIR BACK
Row 1: Ch 267, dc in ninth ch from hook *(first mesh made)*, **mesh** *(see Special Stitches)* across, turn. *(87 mesh made)*
Row 2: Beg mesh *(see Special Stitches)*, mesh across, turn.
Row 3: Beg mesh, mesh, **block** *(see Special Stitches)* 83 times, mesh twice, turn. *(4 mesh, 83 blocks)*
Row 4: Beg mesh, mesh, block twice, [**lacet** *(see Special Stitches)*, block twice] 9 times, lacet, block 3 times, [lacet, block twice] 10 times, mesh twice, turn.
Row 5: Beg mesh, mesh, block twice, [**double mesh** *(see Special Stitches)*, block twice] 9 times, double mesh, block 3 times, [double mesh, block twice] 10 times, mesh twice, turn.
Row 6: Beg mesh, mesh, block twice, [lacet, block twice] 9 times, lacet, block 3 times, [lacet, block twice] 10 times, mesh twice, turn.

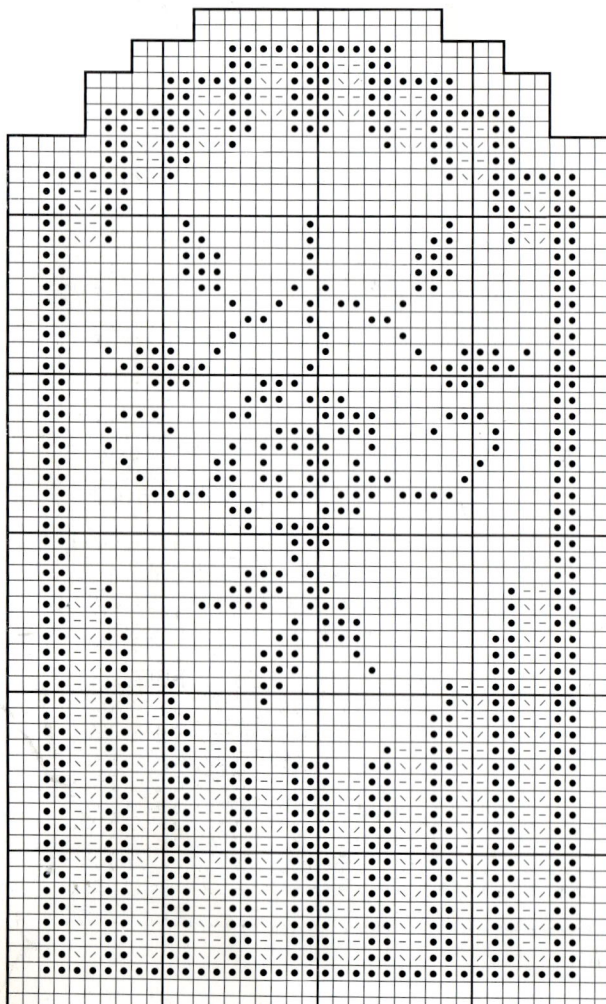

Arm Piece Chart

12 Home Accents in Filet Crochet • Annie's Attic, Berne, IN 46711 • AnniesAttic.com

Rows 7–78: Work according to chart, using Special Stitches as needed, turn. At end of last row, fasten off.

ARM PIECE
Make 2.

Row 1: Ch 123, dc in ninth ch from hook *(first mesh made)*, mesh across, turn. *(39 mesh made)*

Row 2: Beg mesh, mesh across, turn.

Row 3: Beg mesh, mesh, block 35 times, mesh twice, turn.

Row 4: Beg mesh, mesh, [block twice, lacet] 4 times, block 3 times, [lacet, block twice] 4 times, mesh twice, turn.

Row 5: Beg mesh, mesh, [block 3 times, double mesh] 4 times, block 3 times, [double mesh, block twice] 4 times, mesh twice, turn.

Row 6: Beg mesh, [block twice, lacet] 4 times, block 3 times, [lacet, block twice] 4 times, mesh twice, turn.

Rows 7–63: Work according to chart, using Special Stitches as needed, turn. At end of last row, fasten off.

STITCH KEY
- Block
- Mesh/beg mesh
- Double mesh
- Lacet

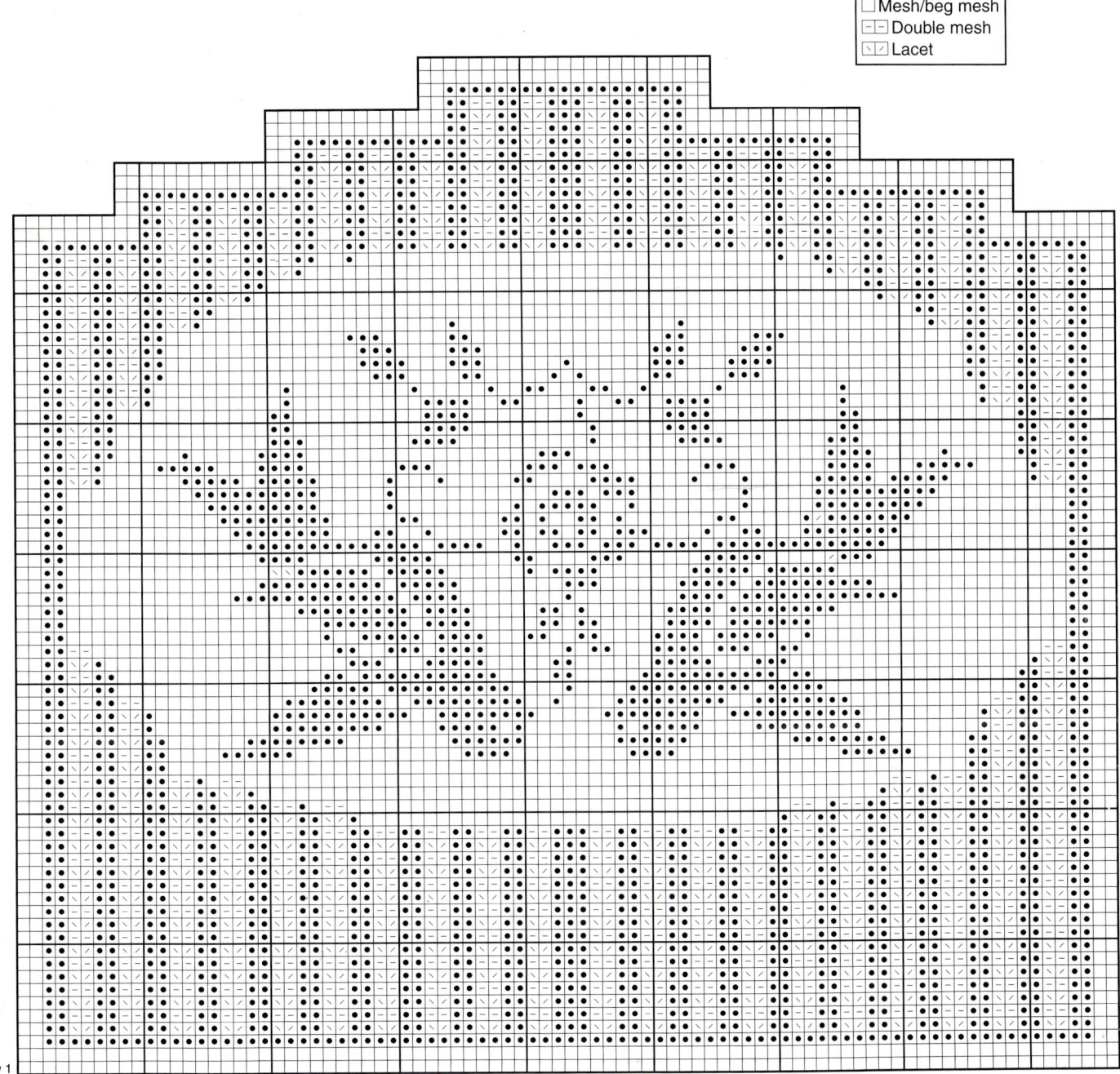

Chair Back Chart

Floral Panel Tablecloth

Design by Nancy Hearne

SKILL LEVEL
■■■□ EXPERIENCED

FINISHED SIZE
63 inches in diameter

MATERIALS
- DMC Cebelia size 10 crochet cotton (284 yds per ball): 20 balls ecru
- Size 7/1.65mm steel crochet hook or size needed to obtain gauge

GAUGE
12 sts = 1 inch; 4 rows = 1 inch

SPECIAL STITCHES
Beginning block (beg block): Ch 3 (counts as first dc), 3 dc in each of next 3 sts, or ch 3, 2 dc in next ch sp, dc in next st.

Block: Dc in each of next 3 sts; **or,** 2 dc in next ch sp, dc in next st; **or,** 2 dc in next pc, dc in next dc.

Block beginning increase (beg inc): Ch 5, dc in fourth ch from hook and in next ch, dc in next dc.

Block end increase (end inc): [Yo, insert hook in base of last dc made, pull up lp, yo and pull through one lp *(ch 1 made)*, {yo, pull through 2 lps on hook} twice] 3 times.

Block beginning decrease (beg dec): Sl st in each of first 4 sts.

Block end decrease (end dec): Leave last block unworked.

Mesh: Ch 2, sk next 2 sts or chs, dc in next st, or ch 2, sk next pc, dc in next dc.

Double mesh: Ch 2, sk next 2 chs, dc in next ch, ch 2, sk next 2 chs, dc in next dc.

Popcorn (pc): 5 dc in next st or ch sp, drop lp from hook, insert hook in top of first dc, pull dropped lp through, ch 1.

Popcorn block (pc block): Sk next st, **pc** *(see Special Stitches)* in next st, dc in next st; **or,** pc in next ch sp, dc in next st.

Lacet: Ch 3, sk next 2 sts, sc in next st, ch 3, sk next 2 sts, dc in next dc.

Double bar: Ch 5, sk next sc, dc in next dc.

INSTRUCTIONS
PANEL
Make 12.

Row 1 (RS): Ch 18, dc in fourth ch from hook *(first 3 chs count as first dc)* and in each ch across, turn. *(16 dc or 5 blocks made)*

Row 2: Beg inc *(see Special Stitches)*, [**pc block** *(see Special Stitches)*, **mesh** *(see Special Stitches)*] twice, pc block, **end inc** *(see Special Stitches)*, turn.

Rows 3–123: Work according to chart using Special Stitches as needed, turn. At end of last row, fasten off.

JOINING PANELS
With RS facing, beg from lower edge at row 91, join with sl st in end of row, *[ch 5, sk next 2 rows, sc in next row] along side to top edge* *(end of row 1)*, [ch 7, sk next 6 dc, sc in next dc] twice, rep between * along other side to correspond to first side. Fasten off.

Join second Panel as follows: with RS facing, beg from lower edge at row 91, join with sl st in end of row, [ch 2, sl st in corresponding ch-5 sp of first Panel, ch 2, sk next 2 rows, sc in next row on second Panel] across to top edge, [ch 7, sk next 6 dc, sc in next dc] twice, [ch 5, sk next 2 rows, sc in next row] along side to top edge to correspond to first side. Fasten off.

Continue to join Panels in same manner until all 12 are joined; 12th Panel will be joined to 11th Panel and first Panel.

CENTER MOTIF
Rnd 1 (RS): Ch 6, sl st in first ch to form ring, ch 5 *(counts as first*

dc and ch 2), dc in ring, [ch 2, dc in ring] 10 times, ch 2, join with sl st in third ch of beg ch-5. *(12 ch-2 sps made)*

Rnd 2: Ch 3, [2 dc in next ch sp, dc in next dc] around, join with sl st in top of ch-3. *(36 dc)*

Rnd 3: Ch 3, [pc in next dc, dc in next dc, ch 5, sk next 3 dc, dc in next dc] around, join. *(6 pcs)*

Rnd 4: Ch 3, [2 dc in top of pc, dc in next dc, 6 dc in next ch-5 sp, dc in next dc] around, join. *(60 dc)*

Rnd 5: Ch 10 *(counts as first dc and ch 7)*, [sk next 4 sts, dc in next dc, ch 7] around, join with sl st in third ch of beg ch-10. *(12 ch-7 sps)*

Rnd 6: Ch 3, [9 dc in next ch-7 sp, dc in next dc] 11 times, 9 dc in last ch-7 sp, join. *(120 dc)*

Rnd 7: Ch 3, [pc in next dc, dc in next dc, ch 7, sk next 7 sts, dc in next dc] 11 times, pc in next dc, dc in next dc, ch 7, sk last 7 dc, join. *(12 pcs)*

Rnd 8: Ch 3, [2 dc in top of pc, dc in next dc, 8 dc in next ch-7 sp, dc in next dc] 11 times, 2 dc in top of pc, dc in next dc, 8 dc in next ch-7 sp, join. *(144 dc)*

Rnd 9: Ch 10, [sk next 5 dc, dc in next dc, ch 7] 22 times, sk next 5 dc, dc in next dc, ch 3, join with tr in third ch of beg ch-10. *(ch sp made)*

Rnd 10: Ch 1, sc in ch sp just made, [ch 7, sc in next ch sp] 23 times, ch 3, join with tr in beg sc. *(24 ch-7 sps)*

Rnd 11: Joining to center of Tablecloth at narrow end of wedges, ch 1, sc in first ch sp, [ch 3, sl st in next ch-7 sp of Panel, ch 3, sc in next ch-7 sp of Center Motif] around, ending with ch 3, sl st in next ch-7 sp of Panel, ch 3, join with sl st in beg sc. Fasten off.

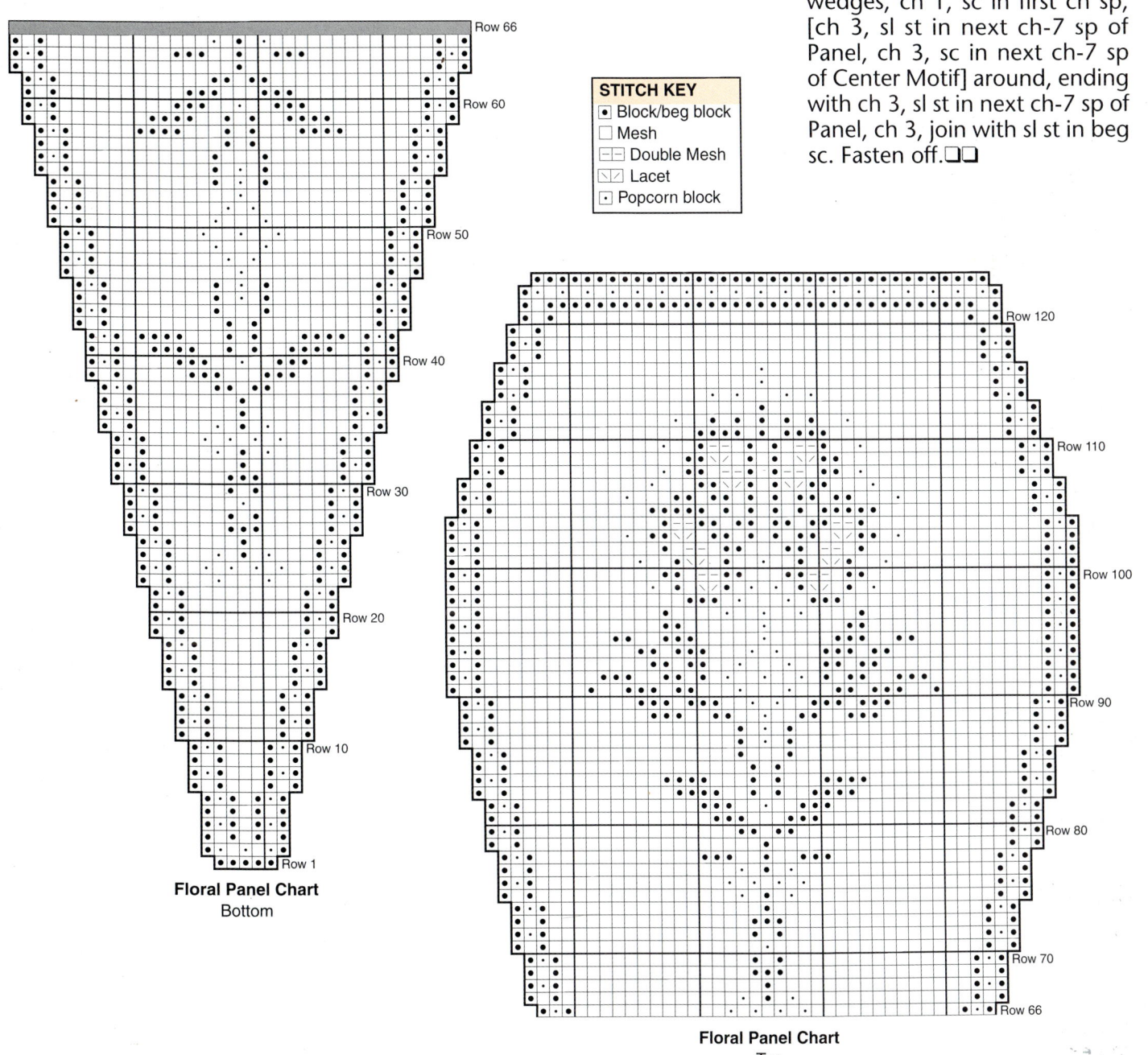

Floral Panel Chart
Bottom

STITCH KEY
- Block/beg block
- Mesh
- Double Mesh
- Lacet
- Popcorn block

Floral Panel Chart
Top

Delicate Curtain Tiebacks

SKILL LEVEL
■■□□ EASY

FINISHED SIZE
4 inches wide

MATERIALS
- Size 20 crochet cotton: 450 yds white
- Size 9/1.25mm steel crochet hook or size needed to obtain gauge

GAUGE
7 mesh = 1½ inches; 7 rows = 1½ inches

SPECIAL STITCHES
Mesh: Ch 2, sk next 2 sts, dc in next st; **or,** ch 2, sk next ch sp, dc in next st.
Beginning block (beg block): Ch 3 (*counts as first dc*), dc in each of next 3 sts.
Block: Dc in each of next 3 sts; **or,** 2 dc in next ch sp, dc in next dc.
Picot: Ch 3, sc in third ch from hook.

INSTRUCTIONS
TIEBACK
Row 1: Ch 48, dc in fourth ch from hook (*first 3 chs count as first dc*)

and in each ch across, turn. (46 dc made)
Row 2: Beg block (*see Special Stitches*), **mesh** (*see Special Stitches*) 13 times, **block** (*see Special Stitches*) once, turn. (13 mesh, 2 blocks)
Next rows: Work according to chart, using Special Stitches as needed, rep rows 2–29 until desired length, ending last rep with row 24.

Edging
Long edges: [12 sc, **picot** (*see Special Stitches*), sk next block, (dc, picot, dc) in next st, picot, sk next block] across long edge. Fasten off.
Rep on other long edge.

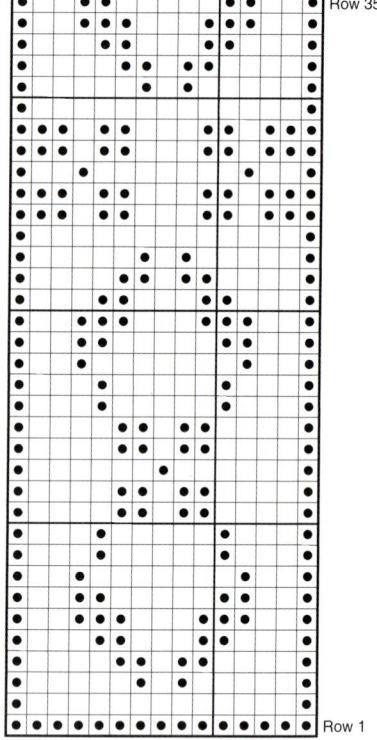

Curtain Tieback Chart

STITCH KEY
● Block/beg block
□ Mesh

Short edge: Sc across, working ch 2, in each corner and joining with sl st to end st on long edge. Rep on other short edge.❑❑

Grapevine Runner

SKILL LEVEL
■■■□ INTERMEDIATE

FINISHED SIZE
21 x 10½ inches

MATERIALS
- Size 30 crochet cotton: 1,000 yds white
- Size 9/1.25mm steel crochet hook or size needed to obtain gauge

GAUGE
6 mesh = 1 inch; 6 rows = 1 inch

SPECIAL STITCHES

Beginning mesh (beg mesh): Ch 5 *(counts as first dc and ch-2 sp)*, sk next ch sp, dc in next dc.

Mesh: Ch 2, sk next 2 sts, dc in next st; **or,** ch 2, sk next ch sp, dc in next st.

Block: Dc in each of next 3 sts; **or,** 2 dc in next ch sp, dc in next st.

INSTRUCTIONS
RUNNER

Row 1: Ch 194, dc in eighth ch from hook *(counts as first mesh)*, [ch 2, sk next 2 chs, dc in next ch] across, turn. *(63 meshes made)*

Row 2: Beg mesh *(see Special Stitches)*, **block** *(see Special Stitches)* 61 times, **mesh** *(see Special Stitches)*, turn.

Row 3: Beg mesh, block, mesh 59 times, block, mesh, turn.

Rows 4–64: Work according to chart, using Special Stitches as needed, turn.

Rows 65–127: Turn chart and reverse design by working back from row 63 to row 1. At end of last row, fasten off.

STITCH KEY
- ● Block
- □ Mesh/beg mesh

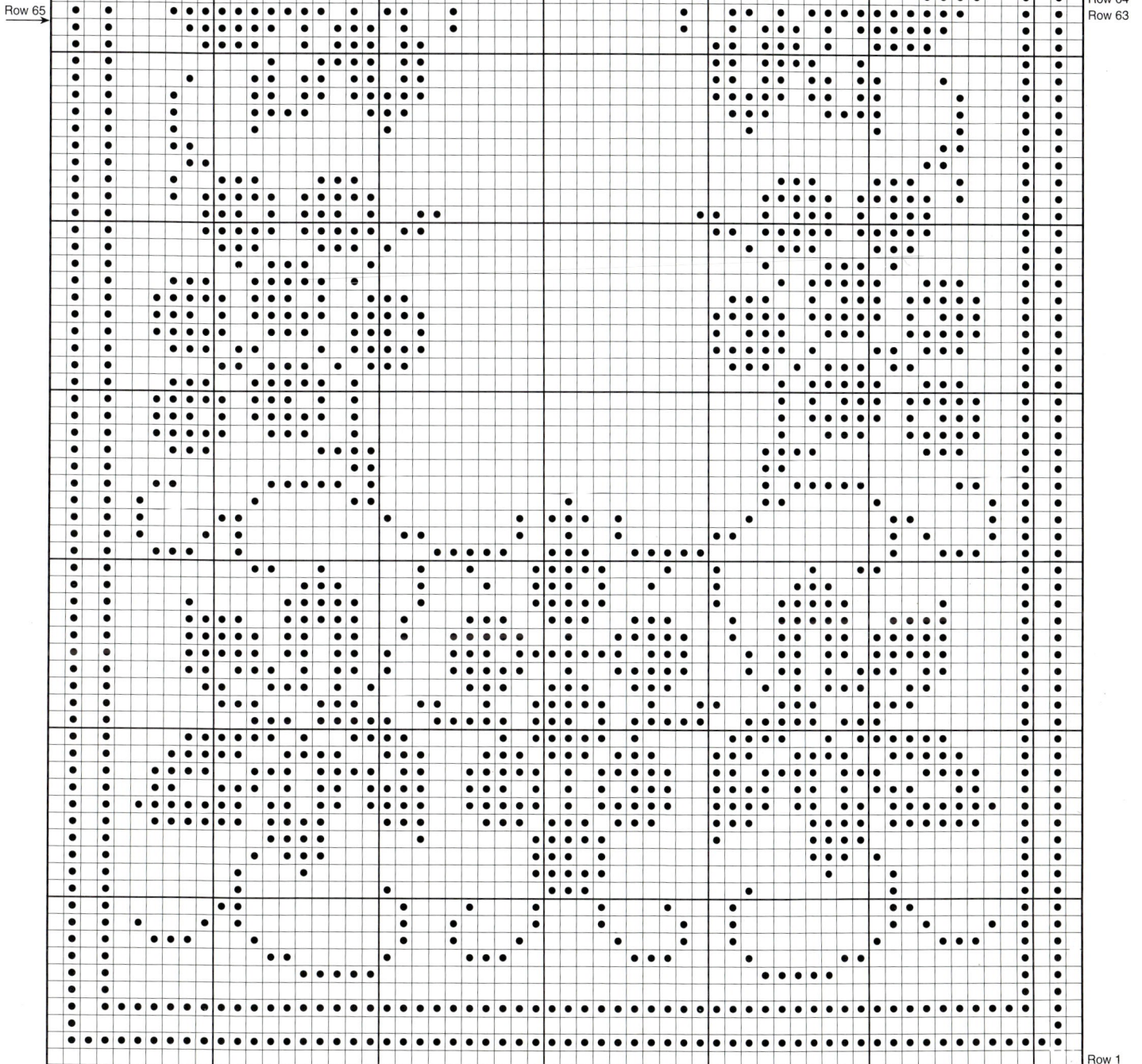

Grapevine Runner Chart

Rose Filet Valance

Design by Vicki Owen

SKILL LEVEL
INTERMEDIATE

FINISHED SIZE
12½ x 31 inches

MATERIALS
- J.&P. Coats Knit-Cro-Sheen size 10 crochet cotton (225 yds per ball):
  4 balls #0001 white
- Size 9/1.25mm steel crochet hook or size needed to obtain gauge
- Embroidery needle

GAUGE
10 sts or chs = 1 inch; 4 rows = 1 inch

SPECIAL STITCHES
Beginning block (beg block): Ch 3 *(counts as first dc)*, dc in each of next 3 sts; **or,** ch 3, 2 dc in next ch sp, dc in next dc.
Block: Dc in each of next 3 sts; **or** 2 dc in next ch sp, dc in next dc.
Mesh: Ch 2, sk next 2 sts; **or** chs, dc in next dc.

INSTUCTIONS
VALANCE
Row 1: Ch 312, for row 1 of graph, dc in fourth ch from hook *(first 3 chs count as first dc)*, dc in each of next 2 chs, [ch 2, sk next 2 chs, dc in next ch] across to last 3 chs, dc in each of last 3 chs, turn. *(103 mesh and blocks made)*

STITCH KEY
- ● Block/beg block
- ☐ Mesh

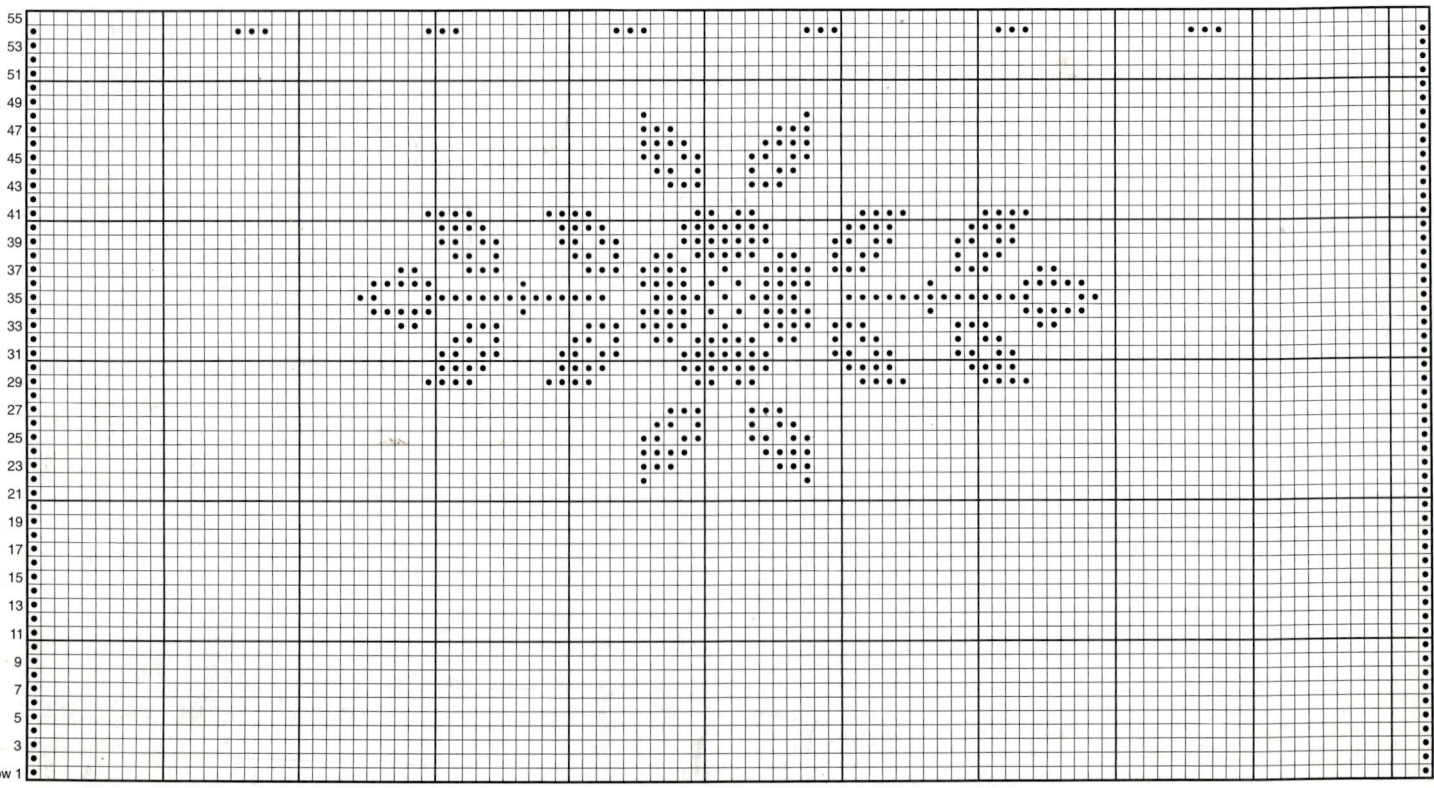

Rose Filet Valance Chart

Rows 2–54: Work according to chart using Special Stitches as needed, turn.

Row 55: For **first scallop**, sl st in each of first 3 dc, **beg block** *(see Special Stitches)*, **mesh** *(see Special Stitches)* 12 times, **block** *(see Special Stitches)*, leave remainder of row unworked, turn. *(2 blocks, 12 mesh)*

Row 56: Sl st in each of first 3 dc, beg block, mesh 10 times, block, leave last block unworked, turn. *(2 blocks, 10 mesh)*

Row 57: Beg block, mesh 10 times, block, turn.

Row 58: Sl st in each of next 3 dc, beg block, block, mesh 6 times, block twice, leave last block unworked, turn. *(4 blocks, 6 mesh)*

Row 59: Sl st in each of next 6 dc, beg block, block 5 times, leave last block unworked, **do not turn**. Fasten off. *(6 blocks)*

Row 55: For **second scallop**, sk next 8 dc on row 54, join with sl st in next dc, beg block, mesh 9 times, block, leave rem of row unworked, turn. *(2 blocks 9 mesh)*

Row 56: Sl st in each of next 3 dc, beg block, mesh 7 times, block, leave last block unworked, turn. *(2 blocks, 7 mesh)*

Row 57: Beg block, mesh 7, block, turn.

Row 58: Sl st in each of next 3 dc, beg block, block, mesh 3 times, block twice, leave last block unworked, turn. *(4 blocks, 3 mesh)*

Row 59: Sl st in each of next 6 dc, beg block, block 3 times, leave rem blocks unworked, **do not turn**. Fasten off. *(3 blocks)*

Next rows: For **third–sixth scallops**, rep second scallop.

Row 55: For **seventh scallop**, sk next 8 dc on row 54, join with sl st in next st, beg block, mesh 12 times, block, leave rem of row unworked, turn. *(2 blocks, 12 mesh)*

Rows 56–59: Rep rows 56–59 of first scallop.

For **casing**, sew starting ch of row 1 to top of row 11.❑❑

Christmas Poinsettias Tree Skirt

Design by Lucille LaFlamme

SKILL LEVEL
■■■◨ EXPERIENCED

FINISHED SIZE
53 inches across at widest point

MATERIALS
- Lion Brand Jamie fine (sport) weight yarn (1.75 oz/176 yds/50g per skein):
  11 skeins #200 white
- Size F/5/3.75mm crochet hook or size needed to obtain gauge
- 3 yds of ¼-inch-wide white satin ribbon

GAUGE
4 mesh or blocks = 2 inches; 5 rows = 2 inches

SPECIAL STITCHES
Beginning increase (beg inc): Ch 6, dc in first dc or tr.
End increase (end inc): Ch 2, tr in same st as last dc.
Beginning decrease (beg dec): Ch 4, sk next st.
End decrease (end dec): Ch 2, holding back on hook last lp of each st, dc in next dc, tr in next dc, yo, pull through all lps on hook.
Mesh: Ch 2, sk next 2 sts, dc in next dc; **or** ch 2, sk next ch sp, dc in next dc.
Block: Dc in each of next 3 dc; **or** 2 dc in next ch sp, dc in next dc.
Lacet: Ch 3, sk next 2 sts or chs, sc in next st or ch, ch 3, dc in next dc.
Double mesh: Ch 5, sk next lacet or 2 mesh or 2 blocks or mesh and block, dc in next dc.
Picot: Ch 5, sl st in dc just made.

INSTRUCTIONS
PANEL
Make 5.
Row 1 (RS): Ch 24, dc in sixth ch from hook *(counts as beg inc)*, [ch 2, sk next 2 chs, dc in next ch] 6

times, ch 2, tr in same ch as last dc *(end inc)*, turn. *(6 mesh, 2 inc)*

Rows 2–44: Work according to chart using Special Stitches as needed, turn.

Rows 45–50: Work according to chart, working sl sts across unworked mesh on rows 45 and 47 using Special Stitches as needed, turn. At end of last row, fasten off.

First Panel Edging
Working along wide scalloped edge, RS facing, join with sl st in end of row 40, ch 3 *(counts as first dc)*, (2 dc, **picot**—*see Special Stitches*, 2 dc) in next row, [ch 2, sc in next row, ch 2, (2 dc, picot, 2 dc) in next row] across edge to and including row 39 on opposite side of Panel; continue around rem sides of Panel as follows: [ch 4, sc in next sp] 39 times, ch 3, dc in same mesh as last sc, (ch 1, dc, ch 1, dc) in each of next 6 mesh, ch 1, dc in next sp, ch 3, sc in same sp, [ch 4, sc in next sp] 38 times, ch 4, join with sl st in third ch of beg ch-3. Fasten off.

Remaining Panel Edging
Work picot edging across wide scalloped edge as for First Panel; for **joining,** [ch 2, sl st in corresponding ch-4 sp on previous Panel, ch 2, sc in next sp on working Panel] across to end; continue around end and opposite side of Panel as for First Panel.

Do not join first and last Panels.

FINISHING
Cut 36-inch length of ribbon. Weave through row 1 of Panels. Pull to gather, tie in bow to close.

Cut remaining ribbon in half. Tie one ribbon in a bow through corresponding ch-4 sps 14 sps below first bow at row 1. Tie second ribbon in same manner 28 ch sps below top bow.

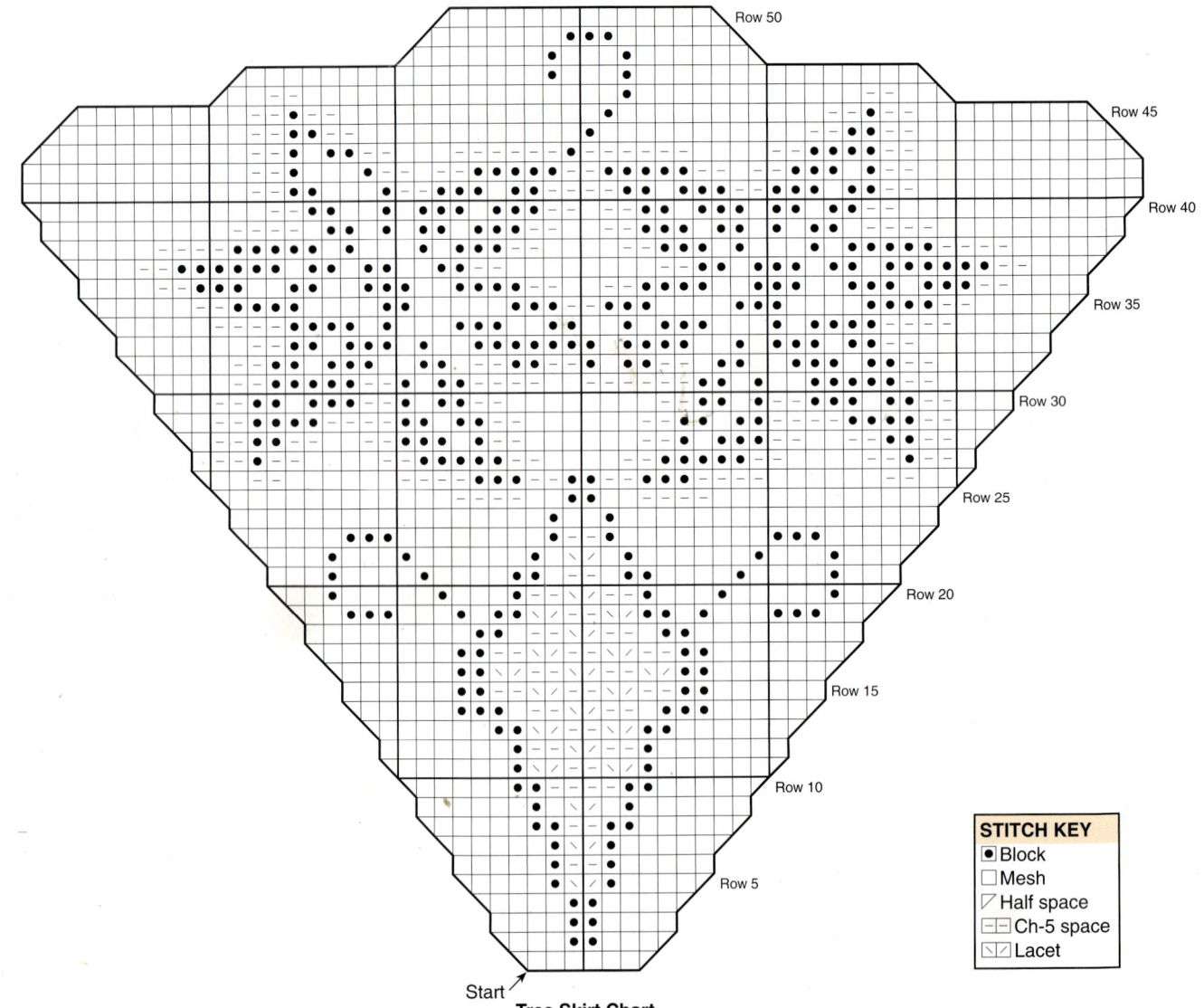

Tree Skirt Chart

Noel Place Mat

Design by Marion L. Kelly and Anne Morgan Jefferson

SKILL LEVEL
 EASY

FINISHED SIZE
11 x 16 inches

MATERIALS
- Coats & Clark South Maid size 10 crochet cotton (400 yds per ball):
    1 ball #0001 white
- Size 7/1.65mm steel crochet hook or size needed to obtain gauge

GAUGE
9 dc = 1 inch; 7 rows = 1 inch

SPECIAL STITCHES
Beginning block (beg block): Ch 3 *(counts as first dc)*, dc in each of next 3 sts.

Block: Dc in each of next 3 sts; **or** 2 dc in next ch sp, dc in next st.

Mesh: Ch 2, sk next 2 sts, dc in next st; **or** ch 2, sk next ch sp, dc in next st.

Picot: Ch 3, sl st in third ch from hook.

INSTRUCTIONS
PLACE MAT
Row 1: Ch 153, dc in 4th ch from hook *(first 3 chs count as first dc)* and in each ch across, turn. *(151 dc or 50 blocks made)*

Row 2: Beg block *(see Special Stitches)*, **mesh** *(see Special Stitches)* 48 times, **block** *(see Special Stitches)*, turn. *(2 blocks, 48 mesh)*

Rows 3 & 4: Beg block, mesh 48 times, block, turn.

Rows 5–42: Work according to chart, using Special Stitches as needed, turn. At end of last row, **do not turn.**

Rnd 43: Now working in rnds, ch 1, sc in top of last dc, **picot** *(see Special Stitches)*, sc in same st, sc in side of same dc, 2 sc in end of next row, *(2 sc, picot, 2 sc) in end of each row across, (sc, picot, sc) in corner, working in starting ch on opposite side of row 1, sc in each of next 5 chs, [picot, sc in each of next 6 chs] across to corner, (sc, picot, sc) in corner, rep from * across side and sts on row 42, join with sl st in beg sc. Fasten off.

STITCH KEY
 Block/beg block
☐ Mesh

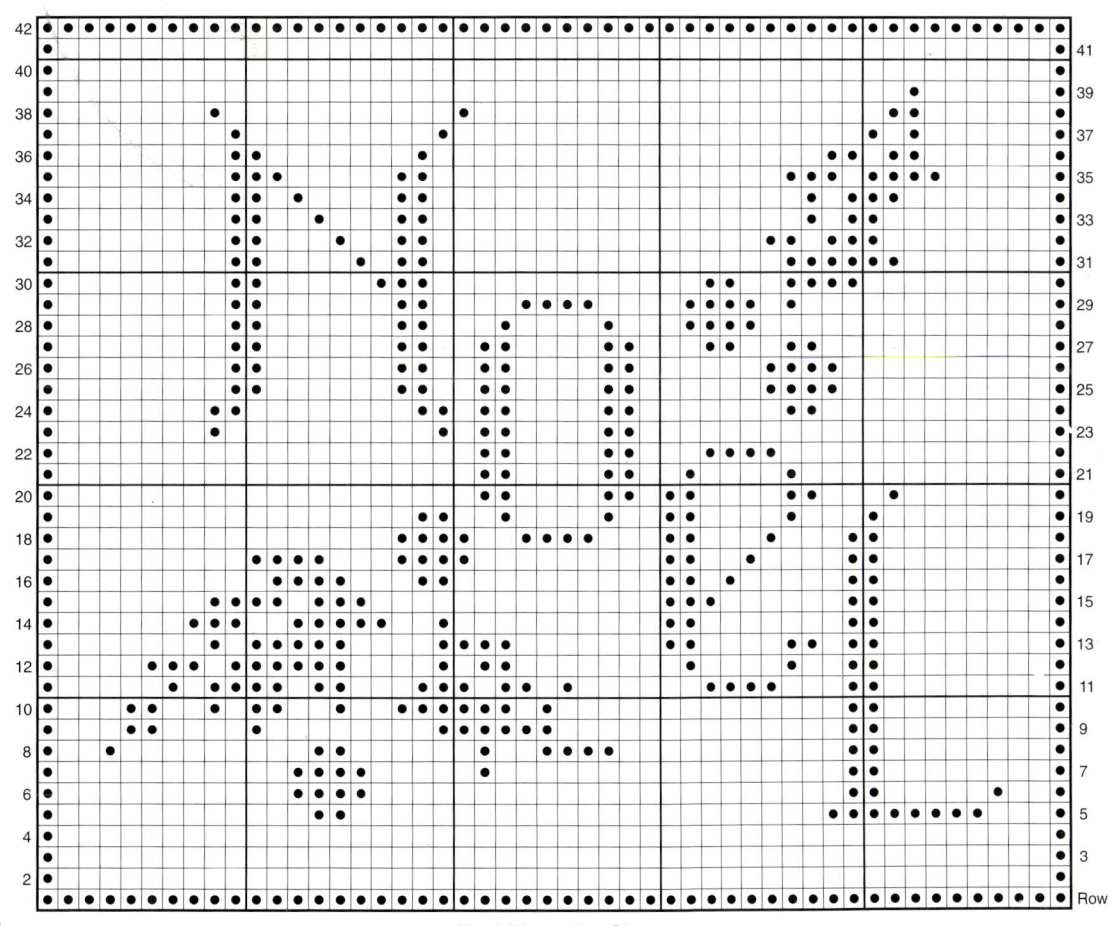

Noel Place Mat Chart

Heavenly Hearts

Design by Sue Childress

SKILL LEVEL
■■■□ INTERMEDIATE

FINISHED SIZE
50 x 62 inches

MATERIALS
- Medium (worsted) weight yarn:
  42 oz/2,100 yds/1191g rose
- Size H/8/5mm crochet hook or size needed to obtain gauge

GAUGE
13 dc = 4 inches; 7 dc rows = 4 inches

SPECIAL STITCHES
Cluster (cl): Yo, insert hook in next st, ch sp or row, yo, pull lp through, yo, pull through 2 lps on hook, [yo, insert hook in same st, sp, or row, yo, pull lp through, yo, pull through 2 lps on hook] twice, yo, pull through all lps on hook.
Beginning block (beg block): Ch 3 (counts as first dc), dc in each of next 2 dc.
Block: Dc in each of next 2 dc, **or** dc in next ch sp, dc in next dc.
Mesh: Ch 1, sk next st or ch sp, dc in next dc.
Cluster block (cl block): Cl in next ch sp, dc in next dc.
Beginning cluster (beg cl): Ch 3, [yo, insert hook in same st, ch sp or row, yo, pull lp through, yo, pull through 2 lps on hook] twice, yo, pull through all lps on hook.

INSTRUCTIONS
AFGHAN
Row 1: Ch 157, dc in fourth ch from hook (first 3 chs count as first dc) and in each ch across, turn. (155 dc made)
Row 2: For row 2 of Angel chart, **beg block** (see Special Stitches), **mesh** (see Special Stitches) 75 times, **block** (see Special Stitches), turn. (75 mesh, 2 blocks)

Rows 3–104: Work sts according to next row on chart, using Special Stitches as needed. At end of last row, **do not fasten off.**

BORDER
Rnd 1: Now working in rnds, **beg cl** (see Special Stitches), ch 1, **cl** (see Special Stitches) in same st, ch 1, sk next st, [cl in next st, ch 1, sk next st] across to last st, (cl, ch 1, cl) in last st, *working in ends of rows, ch 1, [cl in next row, ch 1] across*, working in starting ch on opposite side of row 1, (cl, ch 1, cl) in first ch, ch 1, sk next ch, [cl in next ch, ch 1, sk next ch] across to last ch, (cl, ch 1, cl) in last ch, rep between *, join with sl st in top of beg cl.
Rnd 2: Sl st in next ch sp, ch 3, 6 dc in same sp, *sc in next ch sp, [5 dc in next ch sp, sc in next ch sp] across** to next corner ch sp, 7 dc in next corner ch sp, rep from * around, ending last rep at **, join with sl st in top of beg ch-3. Fasten off.

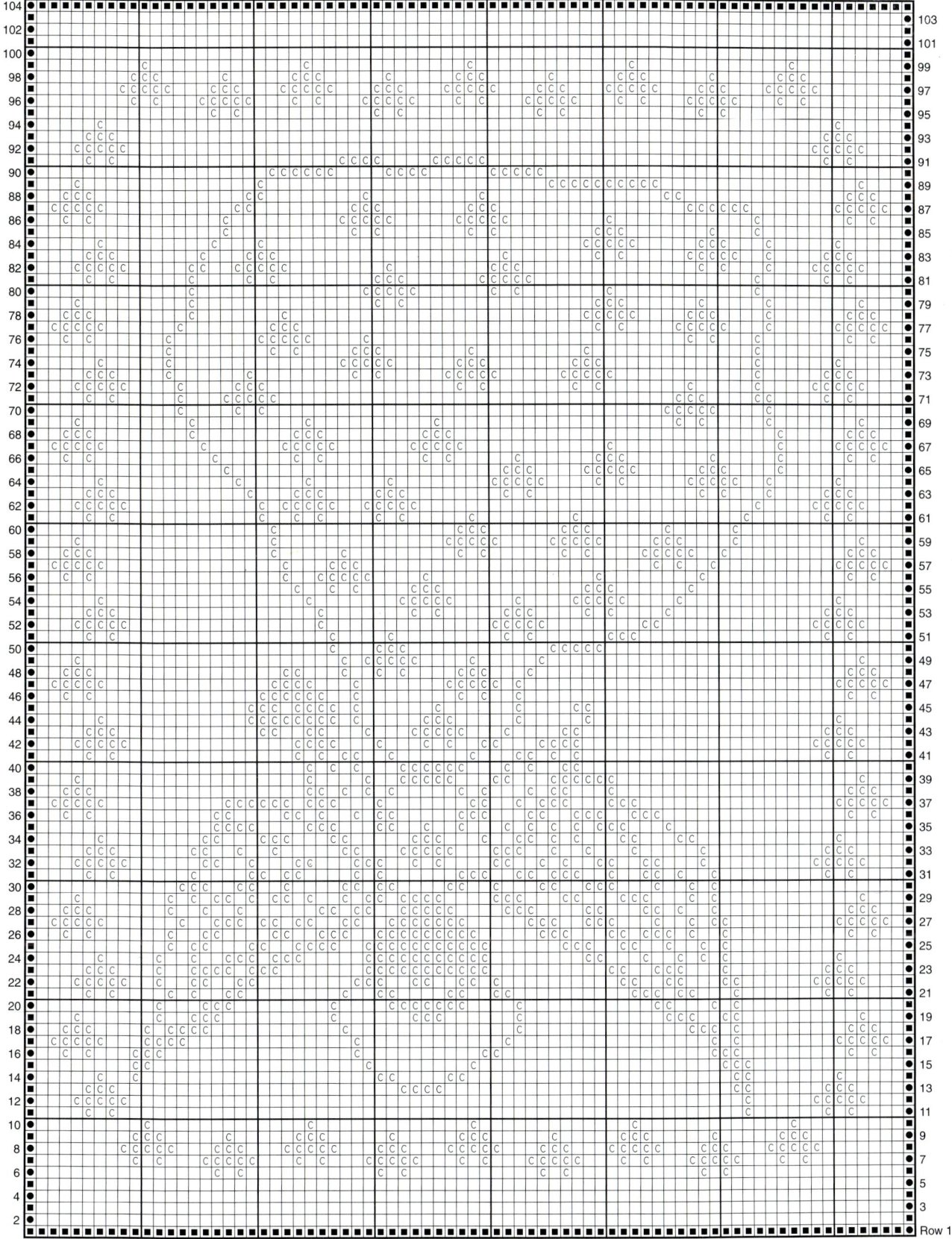

Angel Chart

STITCH KEY
- ■ Block
- ● Beg block
- ☐ Mesh
- C Cl block

Rose Café Curtain

Design by Lucille LaFlamme

SKILL LEVEL
■■■□ EXPERIENCED

FINISHED SIZE
21 x 38 inches, without hanging loops

MATERIALS
- DMC Cebelia size 20 crochet cotton (405 yds per ball): 5 balls blanc (white)
- Size 12/1.00mm steel crochet hook or size needed to obtain gauge

GAUGE
14 dc = 1 inch; 5 dc rows = 1 inch

PATTERN NOTES
For those who chain tightly, a larger hook may be needed to crochet the starting chain.

Work each row on chart from right to left, then return to right on same row.

Work center mesh indicated by gray area of each row only once, **do not repeat**.

Curtain may ruffle until blocked.

SPECIAL STITCHES
Beginning block (beg block): Ch 3 *(counts as first dc)*, dc in each of next 3 sts; **or**, 2 dc in next ch sp, dc in next st.

Block: Dc in each of next 3 sts; **or**, 2 dc in next ch sp, dc in next st.

Mesh: Ch 2, sk next 2 sts, dc in next st, **or**, ch 2, sk next ch sp, dc in next dc.

INSTRUCTIONS
CURTAIN
Row 1 (RS): Ch 539, dc in fourth ch from hook *(first 3 chs count as first dc)* and each of next 2 chs, work according to chart using Special Stitches as needed and rep as stated in Pattern Notes, turn.

Rows 2–105: Work according to chart, using Special Stitches as needed, turn.

Row 106: Ch 1, sc in first st, ch 33, sc in each of next 3 sts, [2 sc in next ch sp, sc in next st] 9 times, ch 33, *[2 sc in next ch sp, sc in next st or sc in each st of **block**—*see Special Stitches*] 10 times, ch 33, rep from * across to last 8 **mesh** *(see Special Stitches)*, [2 sc in next ch sp, sc in next dc] 8 times, sc in each of next 3 sts, ch 33, sc in last st. Fasten off.

Row 107: Working in starting ch on opposite side of row 1 in chs at bottom of sts, with WS facing, join with sc in first ch at bottom of first dc, sc in each of next 3 chs, 2 sc in next ch sp, ch 4, working sc in each dc and 2 sc in each ch sp, [work 6 sc, ch 4] across to last ch sp, sc in next dc, 2 sc in next ch sp, sc in each of last 4 dc. Fasten off.❑❑

24 Home Accents in Filet Crochet • Annie's Attic, Berne, IN 46711 • AnniesAttic.com

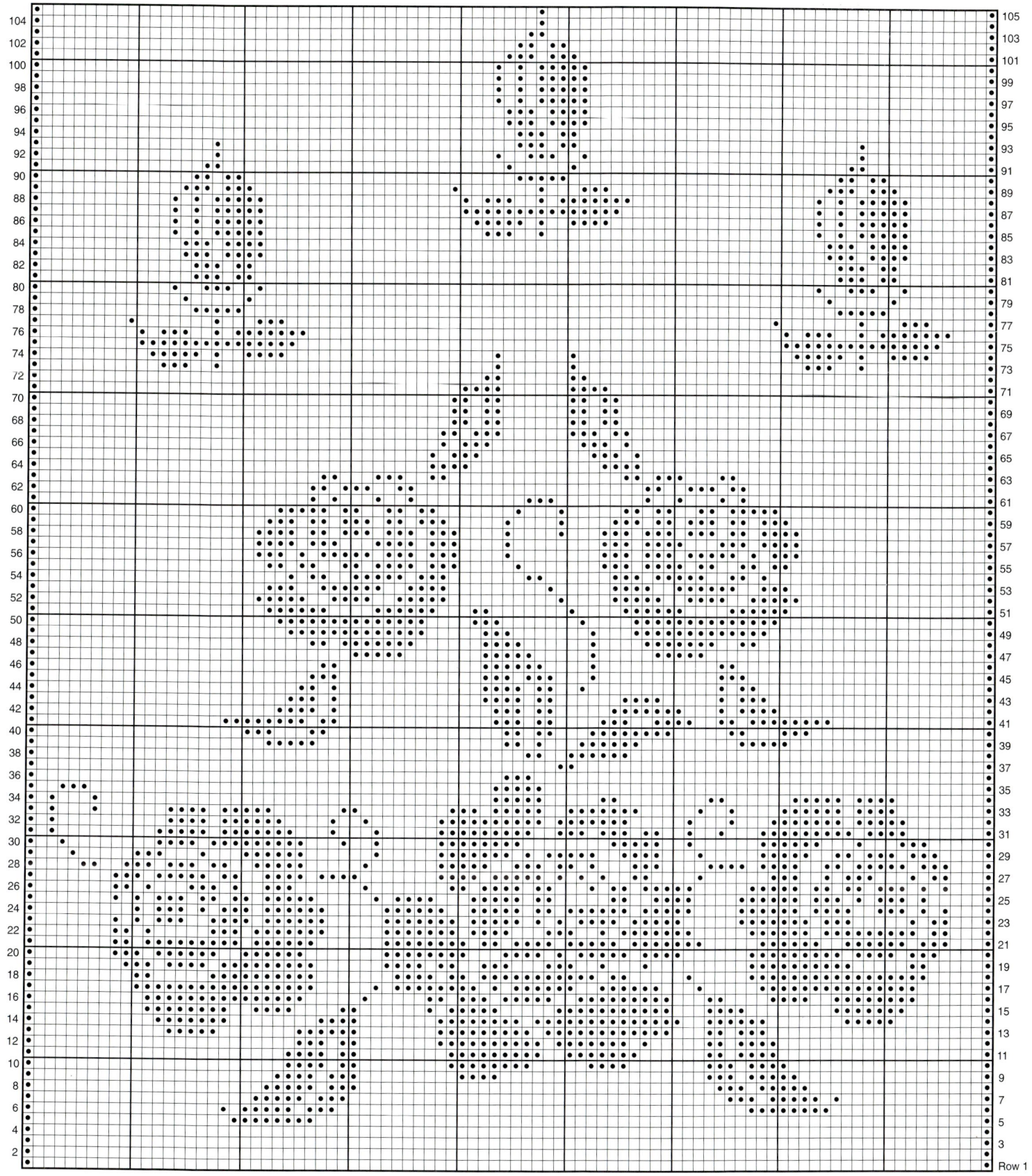

Rose Café Curtain Chart

STITCH KEY
● Block/beg block
☐ Mesh

Annie's Attic, Berne, IN 46711 • AnniesAttic.com • *Home Accents in Filet Crochet* 25

Sweet Dreams Pillow

Design by Elizabeth White

SKILL LEVEL
INTERMEDIATE

FINISHED SIZE
12 x 16 inches

MATERIALS
- Size 20 crochet cotton: 300 yds
- Size 8/1.50mm steel crochet hook or size needed to obtain gauge
- Sewing needle
- Sewing thread
- 2 yds fabric

STITCH KEY
- ● Block
- ☐ Mesh/beg mesh

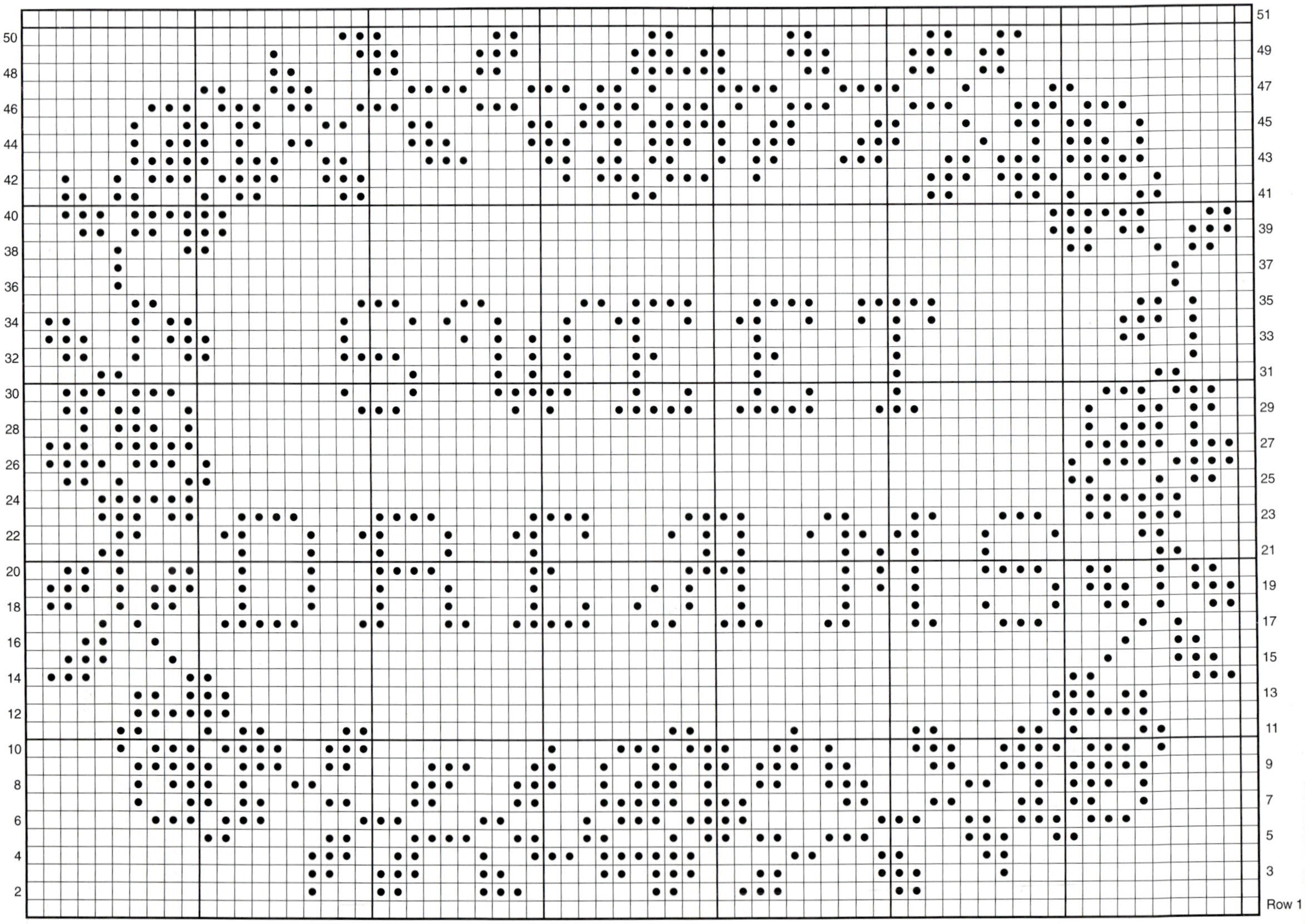

Pillow Chart

26 Home Accents in Filet Crochet • Annie's Attic, Berne, IN 46711 • AnniesAttic.com

- 4 yds of ¼-inch-wide white satin ribbon
- Polyester fiberfill

GAUGE
27 sts or chs = 2 inches; 13 rows = 3 inches

SPECIAL STITCHES
Beginning mesh (beg mesh): Ch 5 (*counts as first dc and ch-2 sp*), sk next 2 sts or chs, dc in next st.
Mesh: Ch 2, sk next 2 sts or chs, dc in next dc.
Block: Dc in each of next 3 sts; **or** 2 dc in next ch sp, dc in next dc.

INSTUCTIONS
TOP
Row 1: Ch 218, for row 1 of chart, dc in eighth ch from hook (*first mesh—see Special Stitches*), [ch 2, sk next 2 chs, dc in next ch] across, turn. *(71 ch sps or mesh made)*
Rows 2–51: Work according to chart, using Special Stitches as needed, turn. At end of last row, fasten off.

PILLOW
1, Cut the following pieces from fabric:
Two pieces each 8 x 72 inches for Ruffle;
Two pieces each 13 x 17 inches for Front and Back.
2, Allowing ½ inch for all seams, sew the short ends of the two Ruffle pieces tog to form a large circle.
3, Fold the Ruffle wrong sides tog matching raw edges and press.
4, Run a gathering thread around the raw edges through both layers. Pull gathering thread to fit around edges of Front, matching raw edges, sew Ruffle to right side of Front.
5, With Ruffle on inside, sew Front and Back right sides tog leaving an 8 inch opening on one side for turning and stuffing.
6, Turn right sides out, stuff, sew opening closed. Sew outer edges of crocheted Top to Front.
7, Cut the ribbon into two 36-inch lengths and two 32-inch lengths.
8, Leaving 10-inch strand at beg and end of each ribbon piece, weave the 36-inch lengths through first and last rows of crocheted Top, weave the 32-inch lengths through mesh at ends of rows on each side.
9, Tie the 10-inch strands in a bow at each corner. Trim ribbon ends.❑❑

Doll Collector's Table Runner

Design by Sue Childress

SKILL LEVEL
■■☐☐ EASY

FINISHED SIZE
10½ x 28 inches

MATERIALS
- Crochet cotton size 10:
    675 yds desired color
- Size 7/1.65mm steel crochet hook or size needed to obtain gauge

GAUGE
7 dc = 1 inch; 3 dc rows = 1 inch

SPECIAL STITCHES
Beginning block (beg block): Ch 3 (*counts as first dc*), dc in each of next 2 sts.
Block: Dc in each of next 2 sts, or dc in next ch sp, dc in next st.

Annie's Attic, Berne, IN 46711 • AnniesAttic.com • Home Accents in Filet Crochet

Cluster block (cl block): Yo, insert hook in next ch sp or st, yo, pull lp through, yo, pull through 2 lps on hook, yo, insert hook in same ch sp or st, yo, pull lp through, yo, pull through 2 lps on hook, yo, pull through all lps on hook.

Mesh: Ch 1, sk next st or ch sp, dc in next st.

INSTRUCTIONS
RUNNER

Row 1 (RS): Ch 61, dc in fourth ch from hook *(first 3 chs count as first dc)* and in each ch across, turn. *(59 dc made)*

Rows 2–79: Work according to chart across, using Special Stitches as needed, turn.

Rnd 80: Now working in rnds in sts, ends of rows and in starting ch on opposite side of row 1, *[ch 3, sk next st, sc in next st] across, ch 3, sk next row, sc in next row, (ch 3, sc) in each row across, rep from *, ch 3, join with sl st in third ch of beg ch-3. *(216 ch sps)*

Rnd 81: Ch 1, sc in each of next 2 ch sps, (dc, ch 1) 4 times in next ch sp, dc in same ch sp, [sc in each of next 2 ch sps, (dc, ch 1) 4 times in next ch sp, dc in same ch sp] around, join with sl st in beg sc.

Rnd 82: Sl st in next st, ch 1, sc in same st, 2 dc in each of next 4 ch sps, [sk next sc, sc in next sc, 2 dc in each of next 4 ch sps] around, join.

Rnd 83: Ch 1, sc in first st, ch 3, sk next st, [sc in next st, ch 3, sk next st] around, join. Fasten off.

STITCH KEY
- ■ Beg block/block
- □ Mesh
- C Cl block

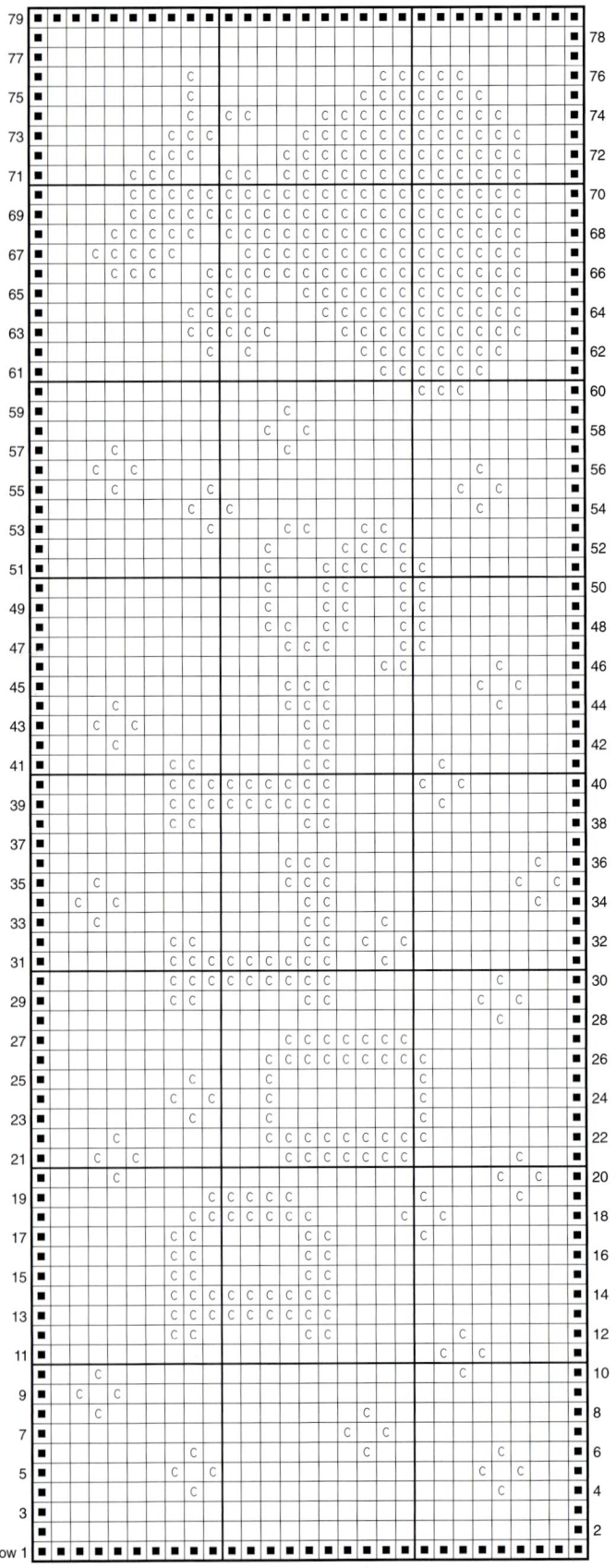

Table Runner Chart

28 *Home Accents in Filet Crochet* • Annie's Attic, Berne, IN 46711 • AnniesAttic.com

Mother's Day Set

Designs by Katherine Eng

PILLOW

SKILL LEVEL
■■■□ INTERMEDIATE

FINISHED SIZE
9 x 10 inches

MATERIALS
- ❏ J.&P. Coats Knit-Cro-Sheen size 10 crochet cotton (225 yds per ball):
    2 balls #1 white
- ❏ Size 10/1.15mm steel crochet hook or size needed to obtain gauge
- ❏ Sewing needle
- ❏ Sewing thread
- ❏ 48 inches (⅛ inch) blue ribbon
- ❏ 12-inch blue ruffled pillow

GAUGE
7 dc = ¾ inch; 2 dc rows = ½ inch

SPECIAL STITCHES
Mesh: Ch 2, sk next 2 sts or chs, dc in next dc.
Beginning block (beg block): Ch 3 *(counts as first dc)*, dc in each of next 3 sts.
Block: Dc in each of next 3 sts; *or*, 2 dc in next ch sp, dc in next dc.

INSTRUCTIONS
PILLOW TOP
Row 1 (RS): Ch 84, dc in fourth ch from hook *(first 3 chs count as first dc)* and in each ch across, turn. *(82 dc made)*
Row 2 (WS): Beg block *(see Special Stitches)*, **block** *(see Special Stitches)* 7 times, [mesh *(see Special Stitches)*, block 4 times] twice, mesh, block 8 times, turn.
Rows 3–30: Work according to chart, using Special Stitches as needed, turn.

BORDER
Rnd 1: Now working in rnds, with RS facing, ch 5, sk next 2 dc, dc in next dc, mesh across, (dc, ch 5, dc) in corner dc, *[ch 1, sk next row, dc in top of st at end of next row] across*, working in starting ch on opposite side of row 1, (dc, ch 5, dc) in corner, mesh across to end, (dc, ch 5, dc) in corner dc, rep between ** once, ending with dc in beg dc sp at end, ch 5, join with sl st in third ch of beg ch-5.
Rnd 2: Ch 1, sc in first dc, *[2 sc in next ch-2 sp, sc in next st] across to corner, 5 sc in corner ch-5 sp, [sc in next dc, sc in next ch-1 sp] across to next corner, 5 sc in corner ch-5 sp*, sc in next st, rep between *, join with sl st in beg sc.
Rnd 3: Ch 1, sc in first sc, *[sk next sc, 5 dc in next sc, sk next 2 sc, sc in next sc] across to corner, 5 dc in center corner sc, [sk next sc, 5 dc in next sc, sk next sc, sc in next sc] across to corner, 5 dc in center corner st, rep from * around, join.
Note: *On the following rnd, in order to come out evenly, adjust at corner by skipping number of sts as needed before corner.*
Rnd 4: Ch 1, sc in first st, [ch 2, sk next 2 dc, (sc, ch 2, sc) in center dc of 5-dc group, ch 2, sk next 2 dc, sc in next sc] around with [ch 2, sc in first dc, ch 2, sk next dc, (sc, ch 3, sc) in center dc of 5-dc group, ch 2, sk next dc, sc

in next dc, ch 2, sc in next sc] at corners, join. Fasten off.

FINISHING
1. Starting at center bottom, weave ribbon through ch sps of rnd 1 on Border around entire piece. Tie ends in bow. Trim ends.
2. Sew onto pillow with white thread through st of rnd 2 on Border.

RUNNER

SKILL LEVEL
■■■□ INTERMEDIATE

FINISHED SIZE
11 x 31½ inches

MATERIALS
- J.&P. Coats Knit-Cro-Sheen size 10 crochet cotton (325 yds per ball):
    3 balls #1 white
- Size 10/1.15mm steel crochet hook or size needed to obtain gauge
- 4 yds (⅛-inch) pink satin ribbon

GAUGE
7 dc = ¾ inch; 2 dc rows = ½ inch

PATTERN NOTE
Cut ribbon as follows:
  two lengths each 48 inches
  two lengths each 24 inches

SPECIAL STITCHES
Mesh: Ch 2, sk next 2 sts or chs, dc in next dc.
Beginning block (beg block): Ch 3 *(counts as first dc)*, dc in each of next 3 sts.
Block: Dc in each of next 3 sts, or, 2 dc in next ch sp, dc in next dc.

INSTRUCTIONS
RUNNER
Row 1 (RS): Ch 90, dc in fourth ch from hook *(first 3 chs count as first dc)* from hook and in each ch across, turn. *(88 dc made)*
Row 2 (WS): Beg block *(see Special Stitches)*, **block** *(see Special Stitches)* 13 times, **mesh** *(see Special Stitches)*, block 13 times, turn.

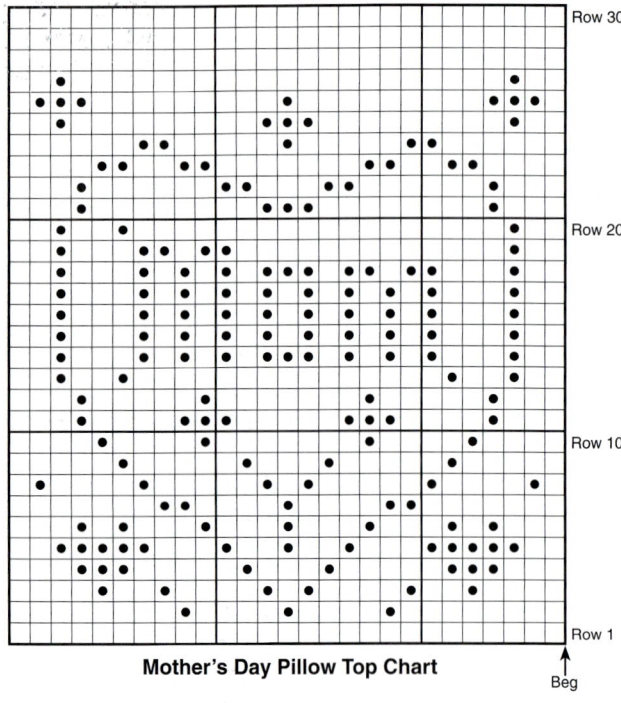

Mother's Day Pillow Top Chart

STITCH KEY
● Mesh
☐ Block/beg block

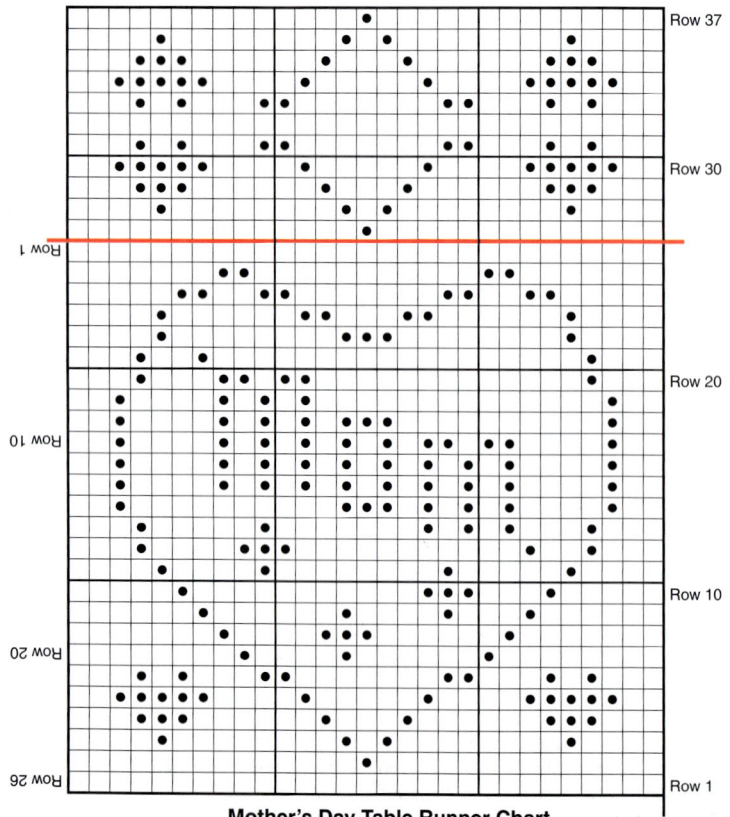

Mother's Day Table Runner Chart

30 Home Accents in Filet Crochet • Annie's Attic, Berne, IN 46711 • AnniesAttic.com

Next rows: Work according to chart, using Special Stitches as needed and working rows 1–26 twice, work rows 27–37 once.

Next rows: Turn chart upside down and work rows 1–26 twice. At end of last row, **do not fasten off.**

BORDER
Rnd 1: With WS facing, ch 5 *(counts as first dc and ch 2)*, sk next 2 dc, dc in next dc, [ch 2, sk next 2 dc, dc in next dc] across to end, (dc, ch 5, dc) in corner dc, [ch 1, sk next row, dc in top of st at end of next row] across, working in starting ch on opposite side of row 1, (dc, ch 5, dc) in first ch, [ch 2, sk next 2 chs, dc in next ch] across with (dc, ch 5, dc) in last ch, [ch 1, sk next row, dc in top of st at end of next row] across, ending with dc in beg sp at end, ch 5, join with sl st in third ch of beg ch-5, turn.

Rnd 2: With RS facing, sl st in first corner ch sp, ch 3, (2 dc, ch 3, 3 dc) in same corner ch sp, ch 1, *[2 dc in next ch-1 sp, ch 1] across, (3 dc, ch 3, 3 dc) in corner ch sp, ch 1, [3 dc in next ch-2 sp, ch 1] across*, (3 dc, ch 3, 3 dc) in corner ch sp, rep between *, join with sl st in third ch of beg ch-3, turn.

Rnd 3: Ch 1, sc in first ch-1 sp, *[ch 3, sc in next ch-1 sp] across, ch 3, (sc, ch 5, sc) in corner ch sp, [ch 2, sc in next ch-1 sp] across to corner, ch 2, (sc, ch 5, sc) in corner ch sp, rep from * around, ch 3, join with sl st in beg sc, turn.

Rnd 4: Sl st in ch-3 sp, ch 1, sc in same sp, *(3 dc, ch 3, 3 dc) in next corner ch-5 sp, [sc in next ch sp, (2 dc, ch 2, 2 dc) in next ch sp] across ending with sc in ch sp just before corner ch-5 sp, rep from * round, join, **do not turn.**

Rnd 5: Ch 1, sc in first st, ch 3, *(sc, ch 3, sc, ch 5, sc, ch 3, sc) in next corner ch-3 sp, ch 3, *[sc in next sc, ch 2, (sc, ch 3, sc) in next ch-2 sp, ch 2] across to corner, (sc, ch 3, sc, ch 5, sc, ch 3, sc) in next corner ch-3 sp, ch 3, [sc in next sc, ch 3, (sc, ch 3, sc) in next ch-2 sp, ch 3] across, rep from * around, join. Fasten off.

FINISHING
1. Weave long length of ribbon through ch sps of rnd 1 of Border on each long side.
2. Weave short length of ribbon through ch sps of rnd 1 on Border on each short end.
3. Cut ribbon ends evenly. Tie ribbon ends in bow. Trim ends.❑❑

306 East Parr Road
Berne, IN 46711
© 2005 Annie's Attic

TOLL-FREE ORDER LINE or to request a free catalog (800) LV-ANNIE (800) 582-6643
Customer Service (800) AT-ANNIE (800) 282-6643, **Fax** (800) 882-6643
Visit www.AnniesAttic.com

We have made every effort to ensure the accuracy and completeness of these instructions.
We cannot, however, be responsible for human error, typographical mistakes or variations in individual work.
Reprinting or duplicating the information, photographs or graphics in this publication by any means,
including copy machine, computer scanning, digital photography, e-mail, personal Web site and fax,
is illegal. Failure to abide by federal copyright laws may result in litigation and fines.

ISBN: 1-59635-008-3   All rights reserved.   Printed in USA   2 3 4 5 6 7 8 9

Stitch Guide

ABBREVIATIONS

beg	begin/beginning
bpdc	back post double crochet
bpsc	back post single crochet
bptr	back post treble crochet
CC	contrasting color
ch	chain stitch
ch-	refers to chain or space previously made (i.e. ch-1 space)
ch sp	chain space
cl	cluster
cm	centimeter(s)
dc	double crochet
dec	decrease/decreases/decreasing
dtr	double treble crochet
fpdc	front post double crochet
fpsc	front post single crochet
fptr	front post treble crochet
g	grams
hdc	half double crochet
inc	increase/increases/increasing
lp(s)	loop(s)
MC	main color
mm	millimeter(s)
oz	ounce(s)
pc	popcorn
rem	remain/remaining
rep	repeat(s)
rnd(s)	round(s)
RS	right side
sc	single crochet
sk	skip(ped)
sl st	slip stitch
sp(s)	space(s)
st(s)	stitch(es)
tog	together
tr	treble crochet
trtr	triple treble
WS	wrong side
yd(s)	yard(s)
yo	yarn over

Chain—ch: Yo, pull through lp on hook.

Slip stitch—sl st: Insert hook in st, yo, pull through both lps on hook.

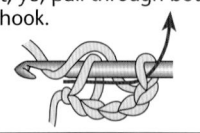

Single crochet—sc: Insert hook in st, yo, pull through st, yo, pull through both lps on hook.

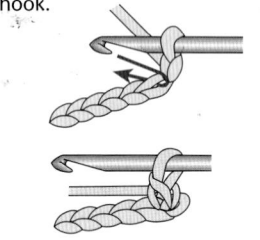

**Front loop—front lp
Back loop—back lp**

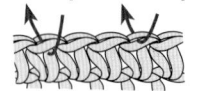

Front post stitch—fp: Back post stitch—bp: When working post st, insert hook from right to left around post st on previous row.

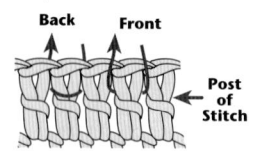

Half double crochet—hdc: Yo, insert hook in st, yo, pull through st, yo, pull through all 3 lps on hook.

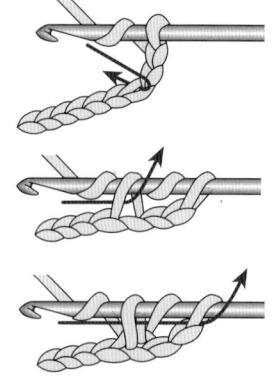

Double crochet—dc: Yo, insert hook in st, yo, pull through st, [yo, pull through 2 lps] twice.

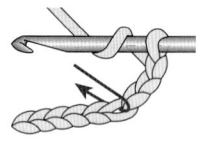
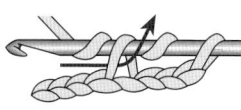
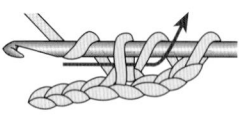
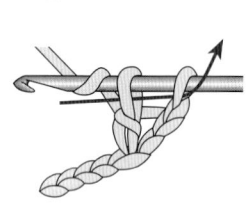

Change colors: Drop first color; with second color, pull through last 2 lps of st.

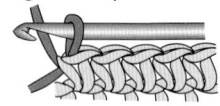

Treble crochet—tr: Yo 2 times, insert hook in st, yo, pull through st, [yo, pull through 2 lps] 3 times.

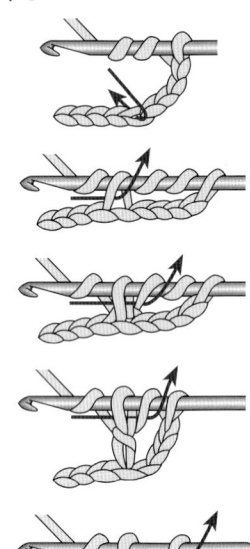

Double treble crochet—dtr: Yo 3 times, insert hook in st, yo, pull through st, [yo, pull through 2 lps] 4 times.

Single crochet decrease (sc dec): (Insert hook, yo, draw up a lp) in each of the sts indicated, yo, draw through all lps on hook.

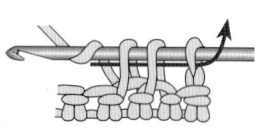
Example of 2-sc dec

Half double crochet decrease (hdc dec): (Yo, insert hook, yo, draw lp through) in each of the sts indicated, yo, draw through all lps on hook.

Example of 2-hdc dec

Double crochet decrease (dc dec): (Yo, insert hook, yo, draw lp through, yo, draw through 2 lps on hook) in each of the sts indicated, yo, draw through all lps on hook.

Example of 2-dc dec

US	=	UK
sl st (slip stitch)	=	sc (single crochet)
sc (single crochet)	=	dc (double crochet)
hdc (half double crochet)	=	htr (half treble crochet)
dc (double crochet)	=	tr (treble crochet)
tr (treble crochet)	=	dtr (double treble crochet)
dtr (double treble crochet)	=	ttr (triple treble crochet)
skip	=	miss

For more complete information, visit

StitchGuide.com